Recollections About the Life
of the
First Ukrainian Settlers in Canada

Collected and Written by

William A. Czumer

Translation by Louis T. Laychuk

Introduction by Manoly R. Lupul

Canadian Institute of Ukrainian Studies
Edmonton 1981

THE ALBERTA LIBRARY IN UKRAINIAN-CANADIAN STUDIES

A series of original works and reprints relating to Ukrainians in Canada, issued under the editorial supervision of the Canadian Institute of Ukrainian Studies, University of Alberta, Edmonton.

Copyright © 1981   The Canadian Institute of Ukrainian Studies
                    The University of Alberta
                    Edmonton, Alberta, Canada

Canadian Cataloguing in Publication Data
Czumer, William, A., 1882–1963,
        Recollections about the life of the first Ukrainian settlers in Canada
        (The Alberta library in Ukrainian-Canadian studies)

Translation of Spomyny pro perezhyvannia pershykh ukrainskykh pereselentsiv v Kanadi

        Includes index.
        ISBN 0-920862-08-X (bound).
        ISBN 0-920862-10-1 (pbk.).

1. Ukrainians in Canada. 2. Ukrainians in Alberta. I. Canadian Institute of Ukrainian Studies. II. Title. III. Series.
FC 106.U5C5713   971'.00491791   C81–091011–X   F1035.U5C5713

Cover: Photo of "The Pioneer Family," a monument by Mr. Leo Mol (Lev Molodozhanyn) of Winnipeg, courtesy of the Ukrainian Heritage Village, near Edmonton.

Printed in Canada by Printing Services, University of Alberta
Distributed by the University of Toronto Press
                    5201 Dufferin St.
                    Downsview, Ontario
                    Canada M3H 5T8

Introduction

This book is a translation of a work first published in Ukrainian by William (Vasyl) Czumer in Edmonton in 1942. It deals with the history of Ukrainian life in Canada during the most difficult period—the first twenty-five years of settlement. Events during the First World War and its aftermath are little mentioned.

It is not difficult to imagine the strong feelings which must have motivated William Czumer in assembling these recollections. The year 1942 marked the fiftieth anniversary of that vanguard of Ukrainian settlers to Western Canada whose coming released a veritable flood of land-hungry peasants from Galicia and Bukovyna in the old Austro-Hungarian empire. In 1941, in the midst of considerable discussion of the anniversary in the Ukrainian press, William Czumer had helped to organize the Ukrainian Pioneers' Association of Alberta, which is still extant. As its first secretary-treasurer, he began collecting data and funds for a book on the Ukrainian settlers of Alberta. To him, it was the first step toward writing the history of the Ukrainians in Canada outlined in an issue of *Ukrainskyi holos* (Ukrainian Voice) in September 1939. (The outline is included near the end of this book.) Both were ambitious projects for a people primarily rural, recovering from depressed economic conditions and plunged suddenly into the uncertainties (and opportunities) presented by world-wide military conflict. As a result, William Czumer found himself with a handful of valuable first-hand personal experiences, numerous photographs and several scattered newspaper accounts which, to the astonishment of many, he proceeded with characteristic vigour and determination to weave into a volume at his own expense.

William Andrew (Andrii) Czumer was born on 5 February 1882 to Andrii and Mariia (née Broda) Czumer in the village of

Drohoyiv, Peremyshl County, Galicia. The extent of his schooling is uncertain but, as the son of the landlord's overseer, it likely included the gymnasium (high school), for Czumer could read and write Ukrainian, Polish and German and was a sergeant in the Austrian army. With his family fairly well established in the Old Country, he alone emigrated to Canada, arriving in Winnipeg in 1903 at the age of twenty-one. After a stint as a railroad worker, he became a member of the first class to enrol in the Ruthenian Training School established in Winnipeg in 1905 by the Government of Manitoba to provide a three-year course for, as Czumer himself put it, "young, intelligent Ukrainian boys who already had some secondary education in their own language but no opportunity to learn English because they lacked finances" (p. 65). The goal was to prepare teachers for schools in the Ukrainian settlements and, besides literacy in the mother tongue, other qualifications were modest: an aptitude for and a willingness to learn English, familiarity with Manitoba's basic elementary school curriculum through grade eight, sufficient integrity for the government to believe that the original costs of lodging and food would gradually be recovered through monthly payments while teaching, and a concern approaching missionary zeal to raise the Canadian (and, at least to the teachers, Ukrainian) consciousness of the settlers and their children through a vibrant and thriving community school. No attendance at the Normal School was required and there is no evidence that the special third-class certificates issued entitled their recipients to teach in non-Ukrainian settlements in Manitoba or in a school elsewhere.

In Winnipeg the student teachers frequented the homes of such successful Ukrainians as Theodore (Teodor) Stefanyk, a strong supporter of Premier Roblin's Conservative administration, an interpreter (especially at election times) and a school organizer in Ukrainian settlements whose influence would have been a factor in the establishment of the Training School, and an astute politician with some legal training in Europe who, in 1911, was elected to Winnipeg's city council to become the first alderman of Ukrainian origin in Canada. In his home, Czumer imbibed the tenets of the Conservative party, which he supported openly and strongly all his life and which may have influenced events at the Bukowina School in strongly Liberal Alberta in 1913—events in which Czumer was a central figure and to which he devotes much space in this book.

Theodore Stefanyk had married Olena Braschuk and in their home Czumer also came to know his future wife, Lena Braschuk, who had emigrated in 1897 as a two-year-old with her parents from Babynci, Galicia, to Sifton, Manitoba, and who lived with the Stefanyks while completing her education in Winnipeg. They were married in Sifton in 1916.

In the meantime, from 1907 to 1913, William Czumer embarked upon a successful teaching career (mainly in Manitoba), which was as much concerned with community development as schooling. His first position at Bachman School, near Beausejour, was one of the few cases where, because of the school district's heterogenous population, the teacher under Manitoba's bilingual school law of 1897 would have had to instruct in four languages—English, German, Polish and Ukrainian. That he managed is clear from his account of the "'Galician' Christmas concert," his sole personal memoir in the book. From his example, in his own words, "The Ukrainians, who had felt like third-class citizens in the district, stood up straight and raised their heads in pride" (p. 69). That—more than anything else—was the main purpose of schooling for the first Ukrainian-English teachers, and to that end they organized educational associations (*prosvity*), reading clubs (*chytalnyi*), drama societies, co-operatives and community halls (*narodnyi domy*). They were 'their people's' protectors and ultimately their benefactors. But to succeed, they and their people had to be strong, and strength lay in organization. William Czumer understood this very well. In 1907 he helped to organize the Ukrainian-English Teachers' Association in Manitoba and served as its first president for three years. He was also president, then secretary-treasurer, of the Brokenhead Farmers' Trading Company organized by him in Ladywood, Manitoba, in 1910. In 1909 he joined the first executive of the Ukrainian Publishing Company, which in 1910 established the *Ukrainskyi holos* to help arouse the national consciousness of settlers who spoke Ukrainian but shunned the label, accepting Galician, Bukovynian, Ruthenian, Austrian or any other offered by officials.

Such, then, was the background of the man who in the spring of 1913 came to Alberta to assume a teaching post at the Bukowina School, near present-day Andrew. The province was in the midst of an election, and even if Ukrainian interests had not required opposition to the Liberal party, Czumer's loyalty to the

Conservatives might have spurred it on. For years, the Liberals, who had manipulated the Ukrainian vote very effectively, had managed to withstand the pressures of prominent Liberal leaders like Peter Svarich (Petro Zvarych) and Andrew (Andrii) Shandro for bilingual schools similar to those in Manitoba. It is not hard to imagine how much classrooms in the hands of veterans of the Boer War or English-speaking summer students incapable of relating to the community must have displeased William Czumer. By suppressing all that was Ukrainian, such teachers reinforced the inferiority complex of the settlers and their children. In Manitoba Czumer had taught successfuly under a very different system, and it would not have been difficult for him to conclude that the educational authorities in Alberta were either inexperienced in the schooling of immigrant children or were consciously following the same policy of forced assimilation that was even then being advanced by the Liberals in Manitoba. In any case, it is clear that Czumer became involved in the election in April on behalf of some disenchanted Liberals who ran as independents in several of the constituencies where the Ukrainian vote was significant. In Manitoba, where even admission to the Ruthenian Training School was tinged with political considerations and the opinion of the teacher at election time was sought openly by bewildered Ukrainian voters at the mercy of all political parties, Czumer's act would not have been unusual. In Alberta his political activity was against the government and was therefore as offensive as it would have been against the government in Manitoba.

The reaction of Alberta's government was as swift as it was severe. Robert Fletcher, the supervisor of schools among foreigners in the Department of Education and an official trustee in certain circumstances, removed Czumer and several other recent arrivals from Manitoba teaching in the Ukrainian settlements. When the elected trustees of the Bukowina School transferred Czumer to a hastily-assembled school across the road, J. R. Boyle, Minister of Education, amended the school law to permit only teachers with Alberta certificates to conduct classes. The incident is described at great length in the book, its most striking aspect being the limited commentary, though the presentation leaves no doubt who had been wronged. It is clear that the Bukowina School experience was a bitter one for William Czumer. It is almost the last subject discussed and there is much detail. Moreover, what follows concentrates heavily on assimilation, drawing on a great variety of materials to show how the lives of immigrants and their children suffer from the callous disregard of linguistic and cultural aspirations by the unicultural 'English.' At the time, Czumer could not be expected to appreciate how strong was the sentiment toward Anglo-conformity, even in Manitoba, nor the sense of special pride which Albertans took in their having avoided Manitoba's, and even Saskatchewan's, difficulties over language in the schools through firm provincial policies which practically excluded all languages other than English. And, of course, once the First World War began, all things foreign were submerged by the growing xenophobia of the time. Still, the hurt inflicted in 1913–15 was very real, and its resentment a generation later clearly showed the depth of the pain.

Unable to teach and rejected by the Canadian army because of military service in Austria, William Czumer acquired a homestead at Wahstao near Smoky Lake. With the help of his wife, an active business and community life followed. During the war he sold farm machinery in the Vermilion area and helped promote branches in Radway, Chipman, Innisfree, Lamont, Andrew and Smoky Lake of the Ukrainian National Co-operative Company, established in Vegreville by Svarich and Paul (Pavlo) Rudyk in 1910. During the postwar depression the co-operative movement, overstaffed and overextended financially, gradually gave way to private firms such as the Smoky Lake Mercantile Store, which Czumer himself established in 1921. In Smoky Lake the Czumers worked hard to develop the community. In 1922 Czumer was elected mayor, and he and his wife were also very active in all aspects of the new Ukrainian Orthodox church movement. A church, a community hall and later the Ukrainian Self-Reliance League, with affiliates for women and children, were established to counter the Orthodox Moscophile and Protestant influences (benefiting from the greater social disorganization of settlers on the more marginal lands north of the North Saskatchewan River) and later the secular Moscophile communist movement of the Great Depression.

With the eldest of his children approaching postsecondary school age, William Czumer, in 1938, moved to Edmonton to provide those additional educational opportunities which he had been denied, but which he knew were so important. After a brief period in the second-hand business (furniture mainly), he formed a partnership to establish Merchants' Wholesale, whose success attracted additional shareholders. During the next twenty years, involvement in the Ukrainian Orthodox community was supplemented by a very active role in the Ukrainian Pioneers' Association of Alberta. In 1961, at the age of seventy-nine, he retired from the wholesale and on 2 August 1963 he died, survived by his wife and five children, one son and four daughters.

William Czumer was no ordinary man. A full twenty years before his death and at an age when few in business take much interest in their own memoirs (let alone those of others), he was laying the foundations for the recollections in this volume. They are significant for several reasons. They are the first of their kind, and though the Association which Czumer helped to found has since published two similar, useful volumes in English—*The Ukrainian Pioneers in Alberta* (1970) and *Ukrainians in Alberta* (1975)—neither approaches Czumer's own as a basic primary source either in the depth to which the first twenty-five years are discussed, the importance of the topics covered or the insights offered into the personal and organizational life of the first generation of Ukrainians in Canada.

Czumer's book is significant also for the attention paid to the life of labourers generally and especially to those in the city. With the Ukrainian population primarily rural and its organizational and institutional roots directly related to farming, it was perhaps as natural as it was unfortunate that Czumer's lead in presenting vignettes out of the life of employed and unemployed workers in the coal mines, lumber camps and railway 'extra' gangs—in and out of season—was not followed up until well into the 1970s. Equally informative are those sections which reveal that at least some Ukrainians entered Canada only after five years as indentured labourers in Hawaii and that others, just as desperate, tried rafting down the North Saskatchewan River to reach the Ukrainian settlements. The simple tale of landlord Khodorovsky who loaned his poor farm worker, Stetsko, funds sufficient to migrate to Canada and their subsequent voluntary repayment shows well not only the basic honesty of grateful peasants, but a trusting humanity which asked few questions among some of the fortunate few who owned the most land.

Still, ultimately it is the didactic role which the book has played that raises it above those which followed and preceded it. Written in a language spoken by the people, it was widely read and discussed and more than any other source established Ivan Pillipiw (Pylypiv) and Wasyl Eleniak (Vasyl Ielyniak) as founding fathers of the Ukrainian people in Canada. The two peasants from Nebyliv, Galicia, capably written up by Professor Ivan Bobersky in a 1937 article in *Kanadiiskyi farmer* (Canadian Farmer), caught the popular imagination only after the article was given wide publicity in Czumer's book. (Czumer was also sufficiently well-informed to recognize the important role which Professor Joseph Oleskiw (Osyp Oleskiv) played in directing Ukrainian immigration to Canada, but the reference was brief and not until the definitive study by Dr. Vladimir J. Kaye (Kysilewsky) in the 1960s did Oleskiw acquire the large place which he now holds in the early history of Ukrainians in Canada.)

The same didactic role explains the retention in the book of Czumer's opening and closing sections on the history of Canada. Always the teacher, Czumer provided the historical outline to help educate those of his many peers whose schooling had been brief and frequently sporadic and whose acquaintance with the country they loved and had helped to develop was severely limited, both historically and geographically. To the better educated, the sections were undoubtedly superfluous, but to those to whom English was still barely a language, it was nice to see oneself related to Canada's past in a language one could easily understand.

Great efforts were made to render the translation as faithful to the original as possible. This is always a difficult task, but in Czumer's case it posed special problems, for Czumer wrote much like he spoke, using a rich if not complex vocabulary, liberally strewn with words and passages which in translation convey neither the humour nor the pathos of the original. The end product is not a literary document, but it does hopefully convey something of the directness and clarity with which the more literate wrote and also of the peasants' preoccupation with detail in relating personal experiences. This is not to say, of course, that all that is related or written is necessarily true. Where beginnings are concerned, there are always difficulties and among the many firsts which Czumer cites, there may be errors or at least differences of opinion. The most obvious have been corrected, and, wherever possible, quotations from English-language sources have been checked against the original. The translation, however, is designed to inform;

it is not a critical work based on the research available.

For the original translation, the Canadian Institute of Ukrainian Studies is indebted to Mr. Louis T. Laychuk of Edmonton, a pioneer himself from the village of Shershenivtsi, Borshchiv County, Western Ukraine, where he was born on 28 October 1894 and received his primary schooling. After emigrating to Canada in 1910, he was employed as a railway section-hand, farm labourer, homesteader and tinsmith. Though apparently unknown to one another, Mr. Laychuk recognized the value of Mr. Czumer's work and concluded that the first-hand experiences therein should be known more widely. They were, after all, those of one of Western Canada's first peoples.

The work was first edited by Dr. Alexander Malycky of the University of Calgary, assisted by Miss Orysia Prokopiw. It was further edited by Mr. George Melnyk of Edmonton, whose technical assistance is also gratefully acknowledged. As the general editor of the Institute's "Alberta Library in Ukrainian-Canadian Studies," the ultimate responsibility for the book's final form is, of course, mine. Mr. David Marples, the Institute's editorial assistant, furnished the index.

Like the original, the translation has no table of contents. For the sake of uniformity, all chapter headings in the original have become free-standing sideheads, as there was frequently little distinction between the two. The most relevant illustrations in the original have been used. Transliteration of Ukrainian names into English is according to the modified Library of Congress system used by the Canadian Institute of Ukrainian Studies in all its publications and may be seen in any issue of the Institute's *Journal of Ukrainian Studies*. On first mention, well-known names are cited according to their common spelling in Canada with the correct transliteration in parentheses. Thereafter only the Canadian version is used: thus, Ivan Pillipiw (Pylypiv), Wasyl Eleniak (Vasyl Ielyniak). Others are cited according to their correct transliteration: thus, Vasyl Iatsiv, Iurko Paish, Ivan Hrynkiv. In the case of place names, those in Ukraine are transliterated as cited on the map of Ukraine by V. Kubijovyč and A. Žukovs'kyi (1978), and those in Canada according to common Canadian spelling: thus, Bukovyna for the region in Ukraine but Bukowina for the school in Alberta.

The publication of this book would have been impossible without the co-operation of the Czumer family who furnished data on the life of their late father and most of the book's original photographs. In the belief that William Czumer would have appreciated the establishment of the Canadian Institute of Ukrainian Studies, it has been their expressed wish from the outset that the Institute publish the translation and that such revenues as may accrue be applied to advance further the study of Ukrainians in Canada. The family's generosity is gratefully acknowledged.

Manoly R. Lupul
Edmonton, 1980

Preface

This book was written to commemorate the fiftieth anniversary of the arrival of the first Ukrainian settlers, who came in 1892 with their families from Galicia in Europe to settle the free, uninhabited lands of Western Canada.

It is written for the sons and daughters of these Ukrainians to preserve the first experiences of their fathers and grandfathers in their new adopted land, and it uses the everyday language of the settlers, who then still called themselves *rusyny* [Ruthenians, the ancestral name particularly of those Ukrainians who inhabited Western Ukraine].

From this book, future generations will learn about their forefathers in Canada—where they came from and why, how they lived and what concerned them, what they missed at first, and the difficulties they faced in surviving and raising a new generation in a new land. They will also learn about the hardships that these pioneers endured to achieve all that we now enjoy and of which we are so proud, because Western Canada certainly was not as we know it today. A lot of perseverance was needed to create a land of milk and honey from its wild forests.

This book explains who launched the massive emigration of Ukrainians from Europe to Canada, where the first Ukrainian settlements were in the West, and why so many people came. It also describes some unusual events that happened to the settlers, as well as their social life once their communities were established.

These modest "recollections" were written so that future generations would not blame their hard-working ancestors for being so busy turning this vast bush into a great, productive land that they did not have time to document, even partially, their own achievements, as have other civilized peoples. The work of Ukrainians in the development of Western Canada deserves careful consideration, and the inheritance they have left us should always be treasured and never forgotten.

To them, in every walk of life in Canada, this book is dedicated.

It is neither the work of an historian nor a writer, but the straightforward recollections of the author and others who are in it. It contains only the more significant events that occurred during the first twenty-five years of Ukrainian life in Canada.

The original goal had been a full commemorative book collectively compiled to honour the fiftieth anniversary of Ukrainian emigration from Europe to Canada. Unfortunately, this could not be done.

These recollections were written so that the threads, once so difficult to weave into a single story of Ukrainian life in an adopted country, would not be lost. They were written neither for money nor fame, but only in eternal memory of those who toiled unselfishly and sacrificed their best years in laying the foundations. They began with very little, and so their history begins with a little book. But the time will come when someone will write more about them and better.

The Author

~1~

A Brief Outline of the History of North America and the Colonization of Canada*

Shortly after the discovery of America by Christopher Columbus in 1492, the countries of Western Europe became very interested in the discovery of new lands beyond the seas and began sending their daring mariners to make further discoveries. For example, Spain sent out Columbus for the second time. England in 1497 sent out John Cabot, who discovered Newfoundland and in 1534 France sent out Jacques Cartier, who discovered the St. Lawrence River in Canada. Later, in 1605, Samuel de Champlain sailed into the interior of the country on the same river and discovered the Indian settlements of Stadacona and Hochelaga. In 1606 he colonized both with immigrants from France.

Many other European explorers took part in discovering parts of North America. Every island in the wide Atlantic became a separate country, like the multitude of islands in the West Indies first visited by Columbus. On returning home, these explorers brought back many valuable things, the native peoples—the Indians—included. They told of the fabulous riches hidden in the new lands, and their stories found eager listeners among the wealthy

---

* Although this chapter contains little that is not already well-known, it is retained to show that Mr. Czumer's collection had a didactic purpose for many in his own generation. Errors in the text are not corrected. (Ed.)

merchants who became interested in America and in developing trade with the Indians.

The trade between the European merchants and the North American Indians was extremely profitable. The Indians did not know the real value of European manufactured goods and traded expensive furs for ordinary glittering trinkets of cheap quality.

When the white Europeans first appeared in America, the Indians thought they were white gods; later when they realized how badly they were being cheated, they called them "white devils."

As trade between the Europeans and Indians expanded, so did the number of traders who brought people with them to act as their agents. At the time not only the English, Spanish and French dealt with the Indians, but also traders from other western European countries.

To protect their trade in America the Europeans built trading posts in suitable locations. These were forts for defence against attacks by Indians or white competitors from other countries. Most of the forts were in the hands of England, Spain and France.

The Rise of European Colonies in America

To safeguard its trading interests in various parts of what was still Indian territory, every nation whose traders dealt with the Indians sent out more and more people to America. The majority were criminals serving long sentences, who were used for hard labour at the trading posts. Usually only men were sent. The first families to emigrate from Europe to North America were the English Puritans. In 1607 they settled near the present-day city of Jamestown in the northern part of Virginia in the United States.

From the outset, the single men, whom fate had thrust onto the American continent, mixed with the native Indians, and from the mixed marriages of "white" and "red" came a new people, the so-called "half-breeds." The latter, however, did not create permanent settlements but moved from place to place, hunting like the Indians. The most successful colonizers at the time were the Dutch, who settled in the region of the Hudson River in New York state. But by the middle of the seventeenth century the English colonists surpassed them in numbers.

The competition for trade in America generated jealousy among the different European powers, who began a race to colonize North

America, each with its own people. The result was large, fast-growing colonies of Europeans, with each country attempting not only to seize as much trade as possible but also as much land as it could. The biggest competitors were England, Spain and France, with the other European states less concerned about colonization because of problems at home.

A long, drawn-out war between England and Spain for trade and territory in America followed. When Spain was finally defeated, England immediately attacked France. The last battle for the possession of North America between the English and French armies was fought at Quebec City in 1759. Four years later, France gave up her colonies in North America to England.

The United States of America

England did not enjoy her wealthy colonies for long because, after her victorious war with France, she tried to impose the burden of the war costs on the local colonists through taxation. The colonists objected because they felt the war between England and France was not fought for their benefit but for that of the lords in England. When England stood by her decision and imposed duties on goods imported into America from other countries, the colonists were further infuriated. One dark night in Boston harbour, masquerading as Indians, they boarded a ship loaded with tea from Asia and dumped the entire cargo overboard. When the British government learned of this, it immediately dispatched a military expedition to punish the unruly colonists.

This so angered them that they openly rebelled, after which followed long years of war between them and the English army. Finally, in 1776 the thirteen rebellious and well-organized colonies declared their independence from England and formed a republic, which they called "The United States of America."

Some colonies on the north and northeast coasts, known as New England, took no part in the revolution because they considered it unwise to break away from mother England at a time when the country was young, sparsely populated and liable to fall into the hands of another state. However, the republicans under their leader, George Washington, wasted no time in adding more colonies to the republic and the northern colonies too were forced to give in. Some people who saw Canada as a refuge from the republicans abandoned their property and fled to Canada, where they became known as Loyalists.

Although the United States of America did try to add Canada to its territory from 1812 to 1814, the Loyalists and the Canadians defended Canada so ably that, even though the Americans outnumbered them and even advanced up to Quebec City, the Canadians with the aid of the British army forced the Americans back across the Niagara River. Since then, they have not tried to conquer Canada again, which remains a British colony to this day.

The Intensive Colonization of Eastern Canada

After the loss of her large and wealthy colonies in America, England turned her attention to the north, to Canada, which she began to colonize initially with her own people from Great Britain. Poor people from England were resettled in Eastern Canada at government expense and supplied with the necessary tools for agriculture and construction. They were also given food for a whole year or for as long as they could not support themselves. In addition, the government gave a cash payment to each adult and loans to develop the land. Similar help was given to the Loyalists by the British government for remaining loyal to England rather than joining the American republic.

But when emigration from England to Canada declined in favour of the United States or other British possessions where the conditions and climate were better, England launched a widespread campaign for colonists in such neighbouring countries as Germany, France, Denmark and Scandinavia. To attract as many as possible and to ease the burden of resettlement, the British government paid part of the travel costs. The colonists who came to Eastern Canada were settled on the model of European villages, which was not to be the case later in Western Canada.

British capital for the development of sea ports in Eastern Canada followed the immigrants, and it did not take long for the ports of Halifax, St. John, Montreal and Quebec to rival the ports of Boston, New York and Baltimore in the United States.

Canada as an Autonomous Colony

By the middle of the nineteenth century the population of Canada had grown sufficiently to raise the issue of self-government. Until then, Canada had been an ordinary British colony in which power rested with England. The growing population consisted of different nationalities and religious denominations, some of whom found the British government half-feudal and no longer acceptable. They felt it favoured some and discriminated against others. The dissatisfied colonials demanded reform, but others found the administration perfectly adequate.

The people who favoured reform were called "Reformists" or "Liberals," while those who stood with the status quo were called the "Family Compact" or "Conservatives." For many years the two opposing groups carried on a political struggle. Individuals and companies not only exploited the natural resources of the country but mercilessly exploited the colonists as well. Their complaints went unheeded. In many cases, the victims never lived to see justice done. As the saying went, "To England it's far away and to God it's very high."

The British government in London, seeing that the situation in the colony was deteriorating and wishing to avoid a repetition of the events of 1776 in the United States when mismanagement caused the loss of the colonies, drew up a special statute called the British North America Act by which the colonies in North America could achieve self-government without breaking their ties with England. The Act came into force in 1867.

For Canadians, this remains a special event. Every year there is a national holiday on 1 July to commemorate the date on which the eastern provinces united into a single federation called the "Dominion of Canada." Three years later Manitoba joined and a year after that, British Columbia. It was not until 1905 that Alberta and Saskatchewan entered Confederation.

The first prime minister of Canada was Sir John A. Macdonald, a Conservative who proved to be a wise statesman. The colonists proudly called the members of the new Parliament "The Fathers of Confederation."

The Northwest Territories of Canada

While British Columbia, Manitoba and the eastern provinces were part of the federation, the Far West was viewed as a "no man's land," an unpopulated and unorganized territory. Only Indians lived there and a handful of whites and half-breeds who traded with them. The territory was controlled by the fur traders of the Hudson's Bay and Northwest companies.

The Canadian government divided the western territories into four districts—Assiniboia, Alberta, Athabasca and Saskatchewan—and gave every citizen equal rights. The trading companies lost their former privileges, but not without compensation. The Hudson's Bay Company, in particular, received great tracts of land, namely, sections eight and twenty-six in each township.

From 1882 to 1905 these districts were administered by a governor resident in Regina and by the Northwest Mounted Police, who were the authority in the West until the districts were reorganized into the two separate provinces of Alberta and Saskatchewan.

The Coming of the Railroad to the West

In Eastern Canada the national economy had developed to a significant point and the colony had begun to enjoy prosperity, but in the West, including Manitoba, there was not the slightest sign of progress. The few colonists and half-breeds were unable to develop the economy, because they lacked easy contact with the civilized world. All goods to and from Eastern Canada were transported in the summer by means of rivers and the Great Lakes and in the winter by dogsled. It was an extremely long and difficult journey. The closest trading centre was Duluth in the States and most of the trade was in furs and livestock.

To improve transportation, it was necessary to build a railroad. The Canadian government in Ottawa agonized over this, because the problems of construction were minor compared to the cost. It was necessary for eastern business to expand into the West; the United States was pushing its colonization further into the northwest and taking western trade away from Canada's businessmen, which upset them.

The question of financing and building a railroad was quickly resolved by eastern Canadian and English financiers, who, in 1872, formed a company called the Canadian Pacific Railway (CPR) to connect the port of Halifax on the Atlantic with the port of Vancouver on the Pacific.

While Canadians were still deciding about a railroad from east to west, American financiers were already building one from St. Paul, Minnesota, to Winnipeg in Manitoba. It reached Winnipeg in 1879, a year before the CPR.

Winnipeg: Window on the West

Without even waiting for the railroad from Ontario to Manitoba, Colonists from Eastern Canada were not the only ones to come Manitoba. Whole communities moved west. Some went via the States, while others crossed the Great Lakes and came overland. In the East a call went out to the young, "Go West, Young Man, Go West." Everyone saw a future for them there.

Colonists from eastern Canada were not the only ones to come west. Europeans, too, were excited by the vast expanse of prairie in the Far West, which included Canada and the U.S. The first farm settlement in Manitoba was Portage la Prairie, which eastern Canadian and English colonists established in 1862. An Indian cart trail, which led from Eastern Canada to the Far West, passed through the area and gave travellers a chance to see its promising rich black soil. As early as 1874 Manitoba had begun to receive such European colonists as Mennonites from Russia, Germans from Hungary, and Frenchmen, Swedes, Danes and Icelanders. Most of the Icelanders came to Manitoba in 1887 and settled in Portage la Prairie, Dufferin and Gimli.

The big rush that began in 1874 lasted until 1886, when the best land in Manitoba had been acquired by speculators. Immigration fever then subsided for almost a decade, right up to 1896. The cause of the standstill was disease that broke out among the colonists and half-breeds and decimated the population. The Icelanders who lived in the region of Lake Manitoba and Lake Winnipeg suffered the most. Heavy frost was followed by drought. In addition, the Indians of northern Saskatchewan rebelled against the Canadian government. All this suspended immigraton to Western Canada, diverting it to the northwestern United States.

The crisis that struck the population of Manitoba worried both the Canadian government and the CPR, which faced the prospect of bankruptcy. The members of Parliament, concerned about the fate of the colonists, were even more worried about the CPR's critical situation, because the government was responsible for the railroad.

Up to 1894, colonists from Western Europe and the United States were preferred immigrants, while all other nationalities were regarded as undesirable. Although they were allowed to enter the country and to purchase land, they were considered undesirable under the Canadian Immigration Act and received no such assistance as did the western Europeans. Nor was there any free land for them.

During parliamentary debates in Ottawa the issue of whether it would be desirable and in Canada's interest to solicit colonists in Central and Eastern Europe was raised, because immigration from Western Europe was drying up. The majority of the members were opposed, believing that central Europeans were not suited for pioneering in the West. They were not welcome because, it was claimed, the Slavs were uncultured, lazy and easy-going and lacked initiative for the tasks of pioneer life. They would bring no advantage to Canada and only cause problems. They would be hard to assimilate and would have to be kept on relief and so on.

For some time Parliament debated the question of whether to invite central Europeans to take up free land in the West. Finally, under pressure from the CPR, their patriotism yielded to the demands of business and they agreed. Those who had earlier supported the idea of bringing in central Europeans were vindicated.

While those opposed to bringing colonists from Central Europe succumbed because they believed in the saying "business before pleasure," they nonetheless stipulated that the government not open immigration offices similar to those in Western Europe. The issue was decided in a parliamentary session in 1894, but the law was not proclaimed until 10 September 1895. The decision was made because a federal election was due the following year, when business interests would have a large say. The members of Parliament knew that when big business raised the issue of new colonists for the West, they had at least to meet it half-way. This was all that the railroad companies needed. They immediately opened up their own offices in Central Europe and immigration to Western Canada flowed again, more than ever before. Business boomed for the shareholders.

Winnipeg became the focus of attention not only in Canada, England and Western Europe, but even among Ukrainian peasants in Austro-Hungary and Russia, who pointed to it on the map with their fingers. Thereafter, Winnipeg became not only a window on the West but also a wide-open door. Everyone destined for the West came through Winnipeg. From 1895 to 1915 the pace of immigration never stopped, never slowed down. It turned the West into the granary of Canada and England.

~2~

The First Ukrainian in America

At the beginning of this book, it was shown that the peoples of Western Europe were the first to make their permanent home in America—initially the Spanish, then the French. Some settled on the coast of Nova Scotia, others in Quebec, and in 1607 English settlers came to Virginia and settled near Jamestown. But by the nineteenth century other nationalities had begun to settle the new land.

For the average Ukrainian or central European it is of interest that in 1619 there were already black Africans in North America. They were brought as slaves. The times were such that there was a large trade not only in blacks but whites as well. In many instances, America was populated by political exiles, threatened by imprisonment or death in Europe. The story of the first such Ukrainian political refugee was told by Dr. H.G. Skehar in a 1942 issue of the almanac *Kanadiiskyi farmer* [Canadian Farmer]. It is reprinted here in abridged form:

The Story of Ahapii Honcharenko

Ahapii Honcharenko was born in the village of Kryvyni in the province of Kiev, Ukraine, on 19 August 1832. At the age of eight he started school, and when he finished the elementary grades, he was sent to a seminary to study theology, which he completed in 1853.

In 1857 the Russian synod sent Honcharenko to Greece as its representative in Athens. There he came into contact with Russian revolutionaries who published newspapers in London opposed to the Russian government. His association with them came to the attention of Ozerov, the Russian ambassador in Athens, who had him arrested and deported to Russia. Honcharenko's friends, however, rescued him from the ship returning to Russia. Thus in 1860 Honcharenko found himself in London, England, instead of Russia. He lived there for a year and a half, then returned to Greece. Since he was a theologian, Meletii Lovtsov, Bishop of Korea, ordained him a priest on 25 January 1862.

Honcharenko continued to maintain contacts with the revolutionaries and through them began corresponding with Bakunin. Convinced that it was possible to set up a printing press in America for Russian refugees, he set sail on 18 October 1864 from Izmir, Turkey, on the *Yarrington* and arrived in Boston on New Year's Day, 1865. From there he went to New York, where he served in Greek Orthodox churches. Later the Bible Society hired him as a translator and an expert in Arabic. In September 1865 he married an Italian, Albina Citti.

When the United States bought Alaska from Russia, Honcharenko was asked to come to San Francisco to edit a newspaper for the Russians in Alaska. It was called the *Alaska Herald* and was published half in English, half in Russian. The first issue appeared in March 1868 and contained some of Taras Shevchenko's poetry. In his later years he lived on a farm in the Hayward area, twenty-five miles from San Francisco. He was known to Canadian Ukrainians and had tried to organize a commune named "Ukraine" in California. He was a committed revolutionary and a patriotic Ukrainian who died on 7 May 1916.

The Arrival of Ukrainians in Canada in 1891

While the peoples of Western Europe were already well-established in America by the mid-nineteenth century, the peoples of Eastern Europe, among them the Ukrainians, knew very little about America. The upper strata were informed about the lands across the sea, but the illiterate peasantry knew little—in fact, they had hardly even heard of them. Austro-Hungary and the Balkans were considered part of Central Europe, while Russia and Turkey were thought of as Eastern Europe.

When the Canadian Immigration Act of 10 September 1895 went into effect, steamship companies immediately spread the news about a tremendous, unprecedented opportunity for those in Central Europe to come to Canada for free land. The major advertising was in Austro-Hungary. The aim, it seems, was to attract as many German colonists as possible, because all the immigration literature was in German. Not until 1896 could Ukrainians in Austria get information in languages other than German.

Although rumours had circulated that people were leaving for America, Brazil and Argentina, there was no active campaign aimed at the Ukrainians, nor any agencies to deal with them in either Austro-Hungary or Ukraine in Russia. The following story of how Ukrainian peasants learned about America and subsequently Canada was told by Professor Ivan Bobersky in a 1937 issue of *Kanadiiskyi farmer*:

How the First Two Ukrainians Arrived in Canada

I have received news that Mr. Ivan Pillipiw [Pylypiv], a farmer, has passed away. He was a happy and talkative man, who ended his life merrily because he died at the wedding of two of his relative's daughters in Northbank, Alberta. It was hot and stuffy in the room, so the windows had been opened. He had sat on the sill, leaned over too far and fallen to the ground. He fell so hard that the people who had run out to help him found him dead. The accident occurred on 10 October 1936 and he was buried on the fourteenth. He was seventy-seven.

I would like to tell Ivan Pillipiw's story about his journey to Canada with his friend Wasyl Eleniak [Vasyl Ielyniak] and also quote from Galican court documents about the criminal proceedings brought against Ivan Pillipiw for going to Canada.

It had always been my dream to meet the two Ukrainians whom everyone spoke of as being the first to come to Canada. For this reason I set out on a trip from Winnipeg to see them. I met Ivan Pillipiw on 2 April 1932 in Lamont, Alberta, and the next day I visited Wasyl Eleniak on his farm near Chipman, Alberta.

I wrote down what they told me about their voyage to Canada in 1891 and what they did in this their new home. Eleniak's memoirs were published in Canada in 1933 in [the Winnipeg almanac] *Providnyk* [Leader], the organ of the [St. Raphael's Ukrainian Immigrants'] Welfare Association [of Canada]. Pillipiw's account consists of the interview I had with him. I have omitted my own questions in order to capture the full power of his reminiscences. This is his story:

We were the first two from Nebyliv to come to Canada. The village is near Kalush. I went to school and learned to read and write. In school the teacher spoke of America and Canada, and then later we heard more from Germans who had relatives there. Some people from our village floated logs down the Lymnytsia River and heard talk of Canada, because at this time everyone was talking about this country.

"Have you got the address of your relative?" I asked one German.

"Yes."

"Write it down for me."

"Okay."

Havrey gave me the address of his son and daughter and I wrote to them. I received an answer to my letter, which said, "Leave those mountains and valleys and come here."

"Yes, I'm coming," I wrote back.

I really wanted to go right away. I'd have bread to eat there. I can read and write and I know a bit of German. All in Canada are not that educated. In my village very few could read. But my wife didn't want to go. She was afraid of the ocean and strange places. Every day she'd say to me, "I won't go. I won't go. I won't go."

"Then stay!"

I had married into my wife's household. She was my neighbour's daughter. I sold a team of horses and a yoke of oxen to pay for my steamship ticket, but it looked as if I didn't have enough money for the full fare so I sold some of my land to pay for the trip.

Then my father said to my wife, "Don't go now. Let him go by himself to see what the land is like. Later, we'll see what happens."

When I tried to get a passport at the county seat, I just barely managed to get it. I asked for a passport for both of us, my wife and myself. I don't have it anymore; it burned in a fire on my farm.

I was born in 1859. When I left I had three children—Vasyl, who was eight years old, and Iurko and Nykola, who were both three. Although I did get a passport for the whole family, I left by myself. My wife didn't have enough courage; she and the children stayed home. This was in the fall of 1891.

Three of us went—Wasyl Eleniak, Iurko Panischak, my brother-in-law, and myself. On my advice they went to get passports. They were also from Nebyliv. Both were married but they went without their wives, the same as I. I had gone to school in the village for four years and had a good teacher, but the other two hadn't gone so they didn't know how to read or write. They listened to my advice and set out with me for Canada.

We went through Stry, then Peremyshl and from there to Oswiecim [Auschwitz], where the authorities checked our papers.

"Show us your money," one of them demanded.

I had 600 Austrian crowns, Eleniak had 190 and Panischak 120. The authorities ordered Panischak to return and he was put on the next train to Kalush. The two of us arrived in Hamburg, where an agent put us aboard a large ship for the ocean crossing. We sailed for twenty-two days. The trip was both good and bad. After crossing the ocean, the ship sailed down a river to a big town. It was Montreal.

We got off the ship in the morning and in the afternoon we boarded a train and went across Canada. The trip was a little long—for two and a half days we wended our way past rocky cliffs, forests, lakes and uninhabited land. It was obvious we were in a wild country. We arrived at a town that wasn't very big with wood frame buildings. At the station we were told to get off the train by authorities who spoke our language but who seemed to be Germans, not our own people. This was Winnipeg.

What day we left Hamburg and what day we arrived in Montreal or in Winnipeg, I honestly don't remember. It was in the fall of 1891. I don't have my passport anymore; it burned on my farm at Bruderheim.

At the station in Winnipeg they brought a man who spoke German and also our own language, Ukrainian, as we now say. He had to show us the land and we could go anywhere, because for us the train was free. The agent took us to Langenburg to a farmer's place. I've forgotten his name. Both of us stayed with that farmer for a week. They took us around to see the land so we could choose some for ourselves. Here I met some Germans I knew who had worked under my supervision in the forests of the Lymnytsia.

We liked the farms. I wrote down the co-ordinates of one quarter-section for myself and another for Eleniak because he couldn't write. We returned to Winnipeg and paid ten dollars each for the land which we took as homesteads.

A German who fixed shoes in Winnipeg and who had come from Kalush told me, "It's warmer in Alberta, go take a look."

I went to the land office and told them I wanted to go to Alberta to see the land. "Fine," they said, "we'll give you free train tickets. Go and pick a good piece of land. We've got lots."

We rode to Calgary because there was no railway to Edmonton yet. We made our way to Greenfields. There was land everywhere; land wherever you went, all empty. Just take a plough and start ploughing. Not like in the Old Country, where people worked small, narrow strips or didn't even have a bit of garden. But we didn't see any forest. After that we returned to Winnipeg from Calgary.

There we met some Jews from Russia who told us, "Go to Gretna, Manitoba, and not far from there you'll find good land."

We bought tickets to Gretna and went to take a look. At the station we met some Germans who also spoke Ukrainian. One of them hired us to help with the threshing. There was enough to eat and drink. We spoke with the older people in our own language, but the young ones already knew English. They told us how hard it was in the beginning—for three, four years it was hard but once they had established themselves, things got better.

I decided to go back to the Old Country to bring my wife and children. Eleniak asked me to bring his wife as well, because he wanted to stay and work in Gretna. I thought it would be good to bring more families from our village. They could get land together and wouldn't be as lonely in a foreign country. I reminded myself that we could take a whole township. Do you know what a township is? It has thirty-six sections, with each section having four farms. A whole township has 144 farms and each farm has 160 acres, the equivalent of 113 morgen in the Old Country. So 144 families could live side by side.

I left Gretna on 1 December and on the fifteenth went from Winnipeg to

Montreal and from there to Boston. Here I had to wait five days for a ship. It took about twenty-two days to sail to London. I had to wait two days in London for a boat to Hamburg. From Hamburg I went to Berlin, Oswiecim, Cracow, Krekhovychi. I hired a horse cart to get me from the station to Nebyliv, and on the fourth day after Christmas* I arrived at the village. That was 1892.

People asked me where I had been and what I had seen. I told them about Canada and said, "Run, run from here, because here you have nothing, but there you'll have land free and be your own master." But the people were ignorant. "It's so far across the ocean," they said. One mother wailed away. Even though she had nine children, she wouldn't go. She'd rather let them starve to death with her. People came to my house. It was full of people, each one asking me over and over again, "Where have you been?"

The people couldn't understand how, across the sea, there was free land without any landlords, which one could get for nothing or next to nothing. They listened to what I had to say and were amazed. Word spread among the villages that a man had returned from God-knows-where and wanted to lead people to some place called America and God-knows-where else. One day the reeve, the priest, the village secretary and the pharmacist [a customs official] came to see me. They began questioning me to see if I was telling the truth. They spread a map on the table and told me to stand beside it.

The secretary asked me, "Where have you been?"

I told him, "In America." Very few people knew where that country was, and even today it's hard to convince someone who knows little about the world.

"Which way did you go?" asked the reeve.

I told him, "I went to Cracow, from there to Berlin and from there to Hamburg. Then I sailed across the ocean to Montreal and from there by rail to Winnipeg. I travelled by train and by boat." I stood to one side and talked while they looked at some sort of map.

"Where exactly were you over there?" the priest asked.

I answered, "The country is called Canada. I was in Winnipeg, Calgary and Gretna. Wasyl Eleniak stayed in Gretna at a farmer's."

There was nothing for them to do but to believe me. The reeve said to me, "Watch yourself."

I went to Perehinsko. There I was confronted by a policeman who said, "Pillipiw, be careful or I'll have to put handcuffs on you one day."

"What for?" I asked.

"You'll see! Be careful what you say."

I didn't think much about it. I sat in a tavern and drank beer. I paid for it or else others did, because people were curious and crowded around me. I told them what they wanted to know. I told them, "Run, run away, because here you haven't got any land but there, there is land. Here you're pushed around but there you can be your own boss."

---

* The date referred to is 11 January by the Julian calendar, but even then the dates and times do not add up correctly. (Ed.)

Twelve families got ready to go: Iusko [Iosyf] Paish, Antin Paish, Mykhailo Romaniuk, Nykola Tychkovsky, Stefan Chichak, Iurko Panishchak, his brother Ivan Panishchak and another Ivan Panishchak (their relative), Vasyl Fedyniak, Vasyl Pitsyk, Dmytro Vyzhynovych, Vasyl Seniuk and Mykhailo Eleniak, senior. There were others but I don't remember them anymore. They sold their land and got passports so they could leave. I helped them. I went to Kalush with them and did all I could, and they paid me a little for my help. You couldn't expect me to worry, to lose time, to arrange things the right way for others for nothing. I had a deal with an agent in Hamburg that if I led people to his office and to his ships, I would receive five dollars for every family. That kind of agreement was common in Canada because people have to spend their time; they have to go here and there, and they have to live. Work has to be paid for. But our people aren't smart; they're only raised in villages. They found out I was getting paid for my work and began to gossip.

One day early in the morning a policeman came to my house. I've forgotten his name. He said to me, "Let's go to the reeve."

I followed the policeman to the reeve's. His name was Ivan Hrynkiv. The secretary was there, too. They also brought my brother-in-law because he had been helping me to get people together, although he had never been to Canada. He was helping me the way a brother-in-law should.

The reeve defended us saying we hadn't done anything wrong, but the policeman marched us to Kalush and took us to the police station. They made a report and threw us in jail.

The next day we were led to the courthouse, where a report was presented and a letter from the agent in Hamburg saying I'd get a reward for showing people the way to Canada. I could have chosen not to show them the letter but I didn't think I was doing anything wrong. The judge spoke our language, but he said he couldn't let us go and ordered us to be taken to Stanyslaviv. A different policeman from Kalush took us to the railroad station and rode with us to Stanyslaviv. Neither one handcuffed us but escorted us with a bayonet fixed to his rifle. It took two hours to get to Stanyslaviv and we sat there in jail, as they say, "incommunicado." We had separate cells. Then we went to court. I had a lawyer but I've forgotten his name. I paid him to defend both of us. In the court they questioned us once more.

The judge said to me, "What do you need land for? Haven't you got enough?"

I said, "We don't have enough land."

The judge said, "You're encouraging people to go."

I said, "No, they want to go themselves."

The judge said to me, "Why didn't you keep your mouth shut. You should go yourself and not drag others with you. You've sold out people to the agent. Our most illustrious emperor helped thirty families return from Argentina at his own expense and you want the emperor to help again should something go wrong."

The entire trial lasted about three hours and we were sentenced to a month in jail. While we were in jail, people were leaving for the new country because they had decided to go. Those who left were: Mykhailo Romaniuk, who lives in Chipman, and Mykhailo Eleniak, who also settled in Chipman but died of the flu; Iosyf Paish, who lives in Delph, and Antin Paish, who lived in Myrnam but is dead now; Mykola [Nykola] Tychkovsky, who died in Star, and Dmytro Vyzhynovych, who died in Chipman. They all settled in Alberta except Vasyl Iatsiv, whose son Ivan is well-educated. He farms in Ladywood, Manitoba. He didn't go to Alberta. Other families didn't leave the Old Country right away but came later.

After I finished my sentence, I made plans to get to Canada with my whole family. In the spring of 1893, three days after Easter, we set out. My wife and four children were with me. The youngest, Anna, was six months old. With us came Iurko Panishchak with his wife and two children and Stefan Chichak with his wife and four children.

But before we could go, I had to make some money for the trip. I got a contract to supply logs to a dealer in Odessa for five cents per cubic foot. I hired five men and paid them day-wages. I found horses and used them to pull the logs to the Lymnytsia River, then floated them down the river to the Dniester and then to Odessa. I worked right up to winter in the woods but spent the winter at home.

Our three families went together by way of Lavochne, Budapest, Vienna, Paris and Rotterdam. From there we took a steamship across the ocean and then a river to Quebec. From there we took the train to Winnipeg.

Here I left my family in a rented house, went down to North Dakota to work and came back in December. Some Germans were going to Athabasca so I joined them. In Winnipeg I bought two oxen, a cow, a plough, sacks of flour, sugar and salt and put everything in a railway boxcar. It cost forty dollars and people rode free. That's how I got to Edmonton and from there to Bruderheim, where I took a homestead. I stayed in Bruderheim for six months, then moved to Star, which was then called Edna. Now the name of the station and post office is Star. I've been here since 1903. I took a farm in township 50, range 19, section 22, southwest quarter, 160 acres, west of the 4th meridian in Alberta.

During these long years I've added four more quarters, so now I own five, paid for and registered. I've also bought and sold lots in Edmonton and Winnipeg, sometimes selling them for a profit and sometimes losing on them. Some Ukrainians bought a store from an Englishman for $16,000 in which I bought fifty shares at $25 each. The store managers were Shkraba and Bricks, but it was all lost. Now I don't own any property in Edmonton, but I own fifteen lots in Winnipeg and pay about forty dollars a year in taxes.

My oldest son Vasyl is now forty-eight years old. He owns five quarters and is married and has a son. My son Nykola went to the city as a worker and now lives on what he earns. My daughter Anna married Joseph Pickeles, a German who works at Swift's meat-packing plant [Edmonton]. My son Mykhailo is still a bachelor. He was born retarded and lives in a home for the retarded.

The years go by. I'm seventy-three years old. I'm happy to talk to people over a glass of beer. I'm in good shape but my wife isn't well. She doesn't feel healthy and stays in the house to keep up her strength. We've hired help to look after the farm since it's hard for us to do the work ourselves.

Our people have made progress in Canada and learned a lot. Canada has made progress, too. People used to work with oxen, then horses and now machines. To drive horses is now too slow so people buy cars. Our farmers already have cars for travelling. From Alberta three Ukrainians have been elected, two to the Legislature in Edmonton and one to Parliament in Ottawa. Michael Luchkovich [Mykhailo Luchkovych] is a good speaker. In Manitoba two Ukrainians have been elected. My son Vasyl should be elected. He's a good farmer and has a good education. He knows what farmers need and how to stand up for their rights.

It's not so good in the Old Country. It's gotten worse for our people. People say and newspapers write that the people are being beaten there just like in the days of serfdom. They want our people to stay illiterate. Already young people born in Canada don't know this, but those who came from the Old Country remember what it was like when the Poles pushed us around. How much longer is it going to last?

Professor Bobersky writes further:

I recorded Ivan Pillipiw's words at the office of Mr. S. V. Bahlay, a notary in Lamont, on 2 April 1932. A friend of Ivan Pillipiw's, a farmer from Star, listened to our conversation and helped him remember different things.

Later I took photos of both farmers. At my request, Mr. Pillipiw supplied a driver with a team of horses and a sleigh to take me to his farm. The snow was melting so the sleigh had to cross puddles of water and mud. Further from Lamont the snow was crisp and the sleigh whisked along. In three-quarters of an hour we reached the farm. The farm house was a two-storey building. I found the lady of the house in a well-heated room. She felt very weak and did not want to talk. Her face was pale from illness and her hands had no strength. I explained the reason for my visit, how I had come from Winnipeg to Alberta, and asked to take her picture, then said good-bye. I spoke briefly to Mr. Pillipiw's hired man and to his wife, who held a small child in her arms. The rooms were spacious but untidy. The almanac *Kanadiisky farmer* lay on the table. The yard was big. So was the barn and the stable, even though in Canada farmers get by without them. There was a windmill to pump water and a few horses were roaming around the yard. The whole area was covered in deep snow. A wide road, which ran parallel to the farm in both directions, led to the railway station. Telephone poles ran alongside the road and a line from one of them carried electricity to the house. This distant farm in the midst of a snow-covered expanse was connected to the world. I took a picture of the whole farmstead.

At dusk I returned to the small town. I shook hands with Pillipiw to say good-bye (while I was away he had been talking to his friends over beer), thanked Mr. Bahlay for all his help and then waited at the station for the train which took me to Chipman that same evening. The next day I visited Wasyl Eleniak on his farm. He told his story calmly and sincerely, choosing his words carefully.

At the end of April I went to Europe and found myself in Yugoslavia. It was here that I rewrote my notes of Pillipiw's story, which in various places seemed inaccurate and incomplete. I sent a typescript to Mr. S. V. Bahlay in Lamont, so that he could read it over with Ivan Pillipiw, correct it and add to it. I made it clear it was to be checked and I included seventeen cents in Canadian postage for reply. I waited twelve months for an answer, and on 25 November 1933 I wrote to Mr. Bahlay asking why he had not replied. At my request, Mr. S. Savula of Winnipeg, a friend of Mr. Bahlay's, wrote to him on 17 January 1934. Still no answer. Ivan Pillipiw died this year—1936—and most likely he never had an opportunity to read and correct my notes. Mr. Bahlay has done us a great disservice. Why? I do not know. Perhaps he did not want anybody, anywhere to know a thing about Ivan Pillipiw.

This is the third time this has happened to me in Canada: a person I asked to correct a manuscript has kept it and the stamps and failed to reply. Each time it has concerned a matter of general importance to us all. Would it not have been better to reply, "I've received your letter and will do as you say, but please pay me for my work." This would have been a sign of intelligence, even business sense. What really are we to think of Ukrainians raised in an English dominion who appropriate the important manuscripts of others? I have not in mind those who do not answer their regular mail. There are lots of them among us. English assimilation has yet to teach them that one must answer letters in time, no matter how briefly.

Neither Ivan Pillipiw nor Wasyl Eleniak knew the date they disembarked in Canada. In my letters of 5 and 7 December 1933, I asked the "Association for the Care of Immigrants" [St. Raphael's Ukrainian Immigrants' Welfare Association of Canada] to make inquiries in Ottawa about the date. The Association acted early in 1934 and the ministry of immigration, after the exchange of several letters, replied on 11 July 1934 that on 7 September 1891 on the ship *Oregon*, among other passengers, two "labourers" by the name of W. Illilik and I. Pylypiwsky passed through the port of Quebec en route to Montreal.

There is no doubt that these same names are those of the two Ukrainians from the village of Nebyliv in Galicia, which at that time was under the rule of Austro-Hungary The ship sailed from the port of Liverpool on 28 August 1891. The journey from England to Canada took eleven days. It is likely that Ivan Pillipiw and Wasyl Eleniak came to Montreal from Quebec City that same day, that is, 7 September 1891.

The letter from the ministry of immigration clearly stated that in that same month, September 1891, two more ships arrived with groups of Ukrainians. It would be good to check the passenger lists for the names of Ukrainians who arrived then. The information would be interesting. Meanwhile, Ivan Pillipiw and Wasyl Eleniak, who arrived in the first week of September 1891, may be considered the first Ukrainians to come and settle in Canada.

I managed to obtain a copy of the criminal proceedings (No.468/36, 1892) against Ivan Pillipiw from the district court of Stanyslaviv. The cost of the copy was eight dollars and the contents are as follows:

Ivan Pillipiw, age thirty-two, married, father of three children, Greek Catholic, farmer, testifed before investigating Judge Karatnytsky in the county court of Kalush on 14 May 1892 as follows:

Last year, 1891, I sold part of my land and after paying my debts I had 156 crowns and 50 cents left. With this money I went to America. I paid 10 crowns for the fare to Mylynets, but because I had to have 150 crowns at the border I borrowed 7 crowns from Wasyl Eleniak, and to be on the safe side I also borrowed 20 crowns from Tyt Ziniak, who was turned back because he had only 120 crowns. I paid 10 crowns and a few cents for the fare to Hamburg and, at the end of September, I boarded Wolff's ship and paid 92 crowns for the fare all the way to Winnipeg. In Winnipeg I paid an additional $2.65, the equivalent of 7 crowns in our money, to get to Gretna.

I stayed there a full two months and worked for two dollars a day. My wife wrote and said she wasn't well and wanted to come to America. I had saved thirty-five dollars, which is eighty-seven crowns, and I had thirty-five dollars from Wasyl Eleniak to bring his wife to America, for which he was to pay half my fare. On 3 December 1891 I boarded the train, then the steamship, then the train again, and on 12 January 1892 I returned home.

I got busy selling the rest of my property. I got 600 crowns for it, then I acquired a passport for myself, my wife and three children and was ready to leave for America. I incited no one to go, but when people asked me what it was like and how to get there, I told them what I knew. At that time other farmers decided to go to America and they got their passports without my help. It was the law, however, that you had to have a steamship ticket to cross the border, so they turned to me to get them a ticket. I wrote to Wolff's office because I had travelled on one of their steamships and was informed by them on 13 March 1892 that a ticket for an adult cost 172 crowns, with children five to twelve years old paying half-fare, one to five years old, 58 crowns, and those under a year, 11 crowns.

I explained this to the people who were preparing to leave, and they decided to send twenty crowns per family. These deposits were left at my home by Nykola Tychkovsky, Dmytro Vyzhynovych, Mykhailo Eleniak and Mykhailo Romaniuk. Last week I received a letter, dated 28 April 1892, which had the tickets enclosed.

At the hearing on 20 May, he testified as follows:

When I was returning from America, the agent Wolff or one of his people contacted me and found that I would be returning to America with my wife. He encouraged me to get people, the more the better, to travel on his steamships, for which he would pay me at a rate of five crowns per family. He also told me to order the steamship tickets ahead of time because the border police would allow those with tickets to pass and it wouldn't be necessary for the passengers to show any more money. I collected deposits from the people so they wouldn't go to some other agent, but I had no intention of cheating anyone.

Judge Karatnytsky held the hearing in Kalush from 14 May to 1 July 1892. On the last day Ivan Pillipiw and his accomplice, Tyt Ziniak, a twenty-eight-year-old father of two children, were handed an indictment dated 30 July 1892, based on the testimony of the following witnesses: Mykhailo Romaniuk, 32, father of four children; Mykhailo Eleniak, 33, father of three children; Dmytro Vyzhynovych, 39, father of two children; Nykola Tychokovsky, 48, father of five children; Ivan Panyshko, 30, father of two children; Iurko Roshko, who represented his daughter, Anna, wife of Wasyl Eleniak; also on the testimony of Karol Szczepanski, the policeman, who arrested Ivan Pillipiw and Tyt Ziniak on 12 May 1892. Both remained in jail until the main trial.

The witnesses did not appear at the main trial because they had already left for America. In the court proceedings only America is mentioned, not Canada. Only Ivan Panyshko testified personally, although he was Tyt Ziniak's brother-in-law and had the right to refuse. He testified to the accused's disadvantage.

The police report does not say who complained to the police or who carried out the investigation at Ivan Pillipiw's home on 12 May 1892 and then arrested him and Tyt Ziniak for allegedly inciting people to emigrate to America and embezzling their deposits.

The main trial took place in the district court of Stanyslaviv on 21 July 1892. The prosecuting attorney, Argasinski, charged the accused with fraud. Defending the accused was the counsel for the provincial court, solicitor Mayeranovski, and the tribunal consisted of four judges—Starosolsky, Shankowsky, Shymanovych and Piskozub.

The judges were not aware of the fact that Pillipiw had returned the deposits. They found him guilty because he had not forwarded the money to the steamship offices and had not given receipts for the money he had received. The verdict was equally harsh for both the accused. Each received one month in jail with days without food each week. The inquiry and imprisonment lasted a total of three months and a week. The court evidently wished to frighten those who in the future might want to exploit emigrants.

After serving his sentence, Ivan Pillipiw left with his wife and children for a free Canada. The emigration of Ukrainians from Europe to Canada began in 1891 and from then on people began to differentiate between Canada and America.

When, in 1920, I entered the home of a farmer near Redwater, Alberta, who had come to Canada in 1892, and asked him, "How has it been for you in Canada?" he replied, "God bless Canada. It made me a man. Here I have land, which I didn't have in the Old Country."

Trzic, Yugoslavia
21 November 1936

How News Spread About the Free Land

The commotion started by Ivan Pillipiw among the peasants of Nebyliv, encouraging them to accompany him to the free lands of America, caused such a stir in Galicia that there was not a town or village where they were not talking about the man who had come from America and had urged them to go there.

At first this news seemed like a fairy tale, but as the more inquisitive heard the same thing from other sources, the people of Galicia got more and more interested. But few could even imagine where the lands were because illiterate peasants did not know geography. Some said land was being distributed in Brazil; others said it was in Argentina. But the majority knew that it was in America, some 6,000 miles across the sea.

Such contradictory news confused the peasants, who were determined to seek these lands, and when they wrote for information from the steamship agents, whether in Hamburg, Antwerp or Amsterdam, they did not always receive the same information. Much depended on the agent. If they wrote to one in charge of emigration to Brazil, they were, of course, advised to go to Brazil, while another advised Argentina because lands there were being given away as well. Some even encouraged going to the Hawaiian Islands.

People did not start to refer to Canada until the people of Nebyliv, headed by Ivan Pillipiw, began writing letters from Canada to their acquaintances in Galicia. "Canada" was printed on the postage stamps and, with the picture of the English monarch, Queen Victoria, people concluded there was such a country in America. Until 1894 there were no other Ukrainians in Canada except those from Nebyliv, Kalush County, Galicia.

Early colonists in the Bruderheim district of Alberta spoke of two Ukrainians from Bessarabia who had arrived in the summer of 1891. One of them, N. Koroliuk, was married to a German and settled with his wife's relatives south of Fort Saskatchewan, Alberta. He was a "Shtundist" [Evangelical Christian] and did not associate with Ukrainians. Eventually all trace of him was lost.

As mentioned earlier, all news about the free land in America spread primarily because of the arrest of Ivan Pillipiw for his agitation in Nebyliv. At the time no one other than the people of Nebyliv dared go to Canada. People began to follow the Germans from Galicia to Brazil and Argentina. Some even left for the Hawaiian Islands because agricultural workers were needed on the plantations. Here is what Mrs. Derko, who ended up in Hawaii after setting out with her parents for Canada, said about her stay there:

> I was still a young girl when I went to the Hawaiian Islands with my parents. When we left the village, we intended to go to Canada or Argentina. But in Hamburg my father and others were persuaded to go to Hawaii, because the pay was good on the plantations and there was work for women and even children. Others signed up, so did my father. His name was Dominik Kutsy.
>
> Everyone signed a contract for five years, or else they wouldn't take you. I remember that over two hundred people signed up, children included. And the total number of people on our ship was over two thousand. We were at sea for more than six weeks, until we were fed up. The women cried and said that we were being taken to the next world. It was a very large ship but I've forgotten its name. Along the way there were many stops and the ship unloaded goods and passengers. Our group of eighty families was taken all the way to Honolulu. There we were divided into smaller groups and sent in various directions to work.
>
> I went to school there and learned Portuguese. There were all kinds of nationalities, but the majority were Portuguese, Japanese and Hawaiians. I liked living there very much because the islands had no winter. My parents were very lonely and were anxious to get to Canada because our countrymen were there and they had written that they owned lots of land.
>
> As soon as the five-year contract ended, my father decided to leave Hawaii for Alberta because his brother lived there. And my mother also wanted to go because the letters had indicated that in Canada there was lots of land and many of our own people. In the area we lived in Hawaii eight Ukrainian families remained, while the rest were scattered over

the other islands.

We arrived in Canada at the end of March 1903. We had sailed across the Pacific to Vancouver and from there we went by rail to Calgary and Edmonton. We got off the train in Strathcona.* W.e arrived in light summer clothes because there's no winter in Hawaii, and we were greeted in Edmonton by such a blizzard that we couldn't even stand outside the station for a minute. My father immediately ran to find a store with winter clothing for us, otherwise we would have frozen to death. Luckily, he still had some money left. We cried and complained that father had taken us away from Hawaii to this Siberia. Had we known that Canada would welcome us the way it did we'd never have moved from Hawaii, because it's a paradise compared to Canada. It's always warm.

Mrs. Derko's recollections about the emigration of these unfortunate people are witness to the fact that untold thousands of poor Ukrainian families were lost in various countries overseas. They left home not knowing where they were going or what they would face when the got there. Take the situation of Mrs. Derko and think about it. Where are the Hawaiian Islands, or for that matter Brazil, Argentina or Mexico, or even Western Canada in relation to Galicia? Those who went there in search of a better life were only simple peasants who did not know geography and did not understand foreign languages. Their plight forced many sincere, patriotic intellectuals in Galicia to look into the matter and to find out more about the countries far across the seas to which the Ukrainian peasant-masses were fleeing. The first was Dr. Joseph Oleskiw [Osyp Oleskiv] from Lviv in Galicia.

Dr. Joseph Oleskiw in Canada

In the early spring of 1895 Dr. Joseph Oleskiw left Galicia on his journey to North America to investigate personally the conditions that faced the poor Ukrainian immigrants. First he visited the United States and by July he was in Canada. It was in Winnipeg that he met Ukrainian farmers for the first time. They were Vasyl Iatsiv, Iurko Panishchak, Iurko Roshko, Luka Kulchytsky, Ivan Paish, Dmytro Vydynovych and Hnat Dmytryshyn.

During his travels in Western Canada Dr. Oleskiw visited the first Ukrainian farm settlement at Beaver Creek, Alberta. The

---

* South Edmonton. (Ed.)

following lived there with their families: A. Paish, who lived nine miles east of Fort Saskatchewan; Stefan Chichak; Nykola Tychkovsky; Ivan Pillipiw; M. Pullishy [Pulyshii]; Vasyl Feniak; Mykhailo, Mykola and Fedor Melnyk; Ivan Dobrutsky; Petro and Matey Melnyk.

Dr. Oleskiw was taken to this Ukrainian settlement by Matthias Hack, a German from Josephsburg, Alberta. At the time Dr. Oleskiw visited some German families as well. He stayed two nights at Fred Gabel's near Fort Saskatchewan, overnight at Muller's near Bruderheim, and he also visited H. Hellwig, who was a neighbour of Antin Paish. Hellwig, a German, came from Lviv. Dr. Oleskiw was welcomed by everyone. Those first Ukrainian settlers remembered his visit for a long time afterward. They praised him for being concerned about their fate right from the beginning and for sparing neither time nor work in visiting his poor countrymen in Canada.

Dr. Oleskiw described his trip across the United States and Canada in two booklets entitled *O emigratsii* [About emigration] and *Pro vilni zemli* [About free lands]. They were published at the end of December 1895 by the M. Kachkovsky Society in Lviv.* One copy of *O emigratsii* was found in the library of Theodore Nemirsky [Fedor Nemyrsky], a farmer at Wostok, Alberta. The booklet contains the following headings: "A Comparison of Brazil with Other Countries," "America and Ukrainian Farmers," "The Way to the Sea," "The Sea Voyage," "The Fertile Belt of Canada," "Land Tenure in Canada" and "Observations on a Journey Through America."

Accompanying Dr. Oleskiw on his trip to the United States and Canada was a man named Ivan Dorundiak [Derendiak], a wealthy peasant from the Kolomyia region of Galicia. Like other peasants he had decided to sell his property in Galicia and settle in Canada. He liked the land around Fort Saskatchewan, which was selling for three to five dollars an acre. When he returned, his wife and sons would not allow him to sell his property in the Old Country in order to buy a new farm in Canada, where they would have to start from scratch.

---

* *Pro vilni zemli* was published by the Prosvita Society of Lviv in July 1895 before Dr. Oleskiw's visit to Canada. *O emigratsii* was published upon his return. (Ed.)

The Mass Emigration of Ukrainians from Europe to Canada

Dr. Oleskiw's literature provoked a lot of interest among the peasants of Galicia. They read it with much enthusiasm and curiosity. Then the steamship companies sent out their literature, beautifully produced flyers and pamphlets filled with numerous illustrations and accounts of the natural resources of Canada. They were so skilfully and attractively done that they not only aroused the enthusiasm of the peasants but also appealed to greed. Barely two years after Dr. Oleskiw's visit to America, there began a mass emigration of Ukrainian peasants from Galicia and Bukovyna.

This continuous mass emigration of peasantry alarmed the Austrian authorities and especially the big landowners, faced with the loss of cheap village labour. Despite all efforts to stem the tide, the land-hungry peasants were so interested in Canada's free land that nothing could stop them from going. Not only the poor went, but even the well-to-do who had the resources and money for such a long trip. How could one not go when it was possible to acquire 160 acres of land for only ten dollars. These 160 acres were what lured the peasant to think he could become rich.

The first Ukrainian to own and hold title to land in Canada was Fedko Fuhr from the village of Bysotsko, Iaroslav County, Galicia. In 1894 he went to Canada, then returned, sold his property in the village and with his wife and family went to Canada for good. Mr. Fuhr paid cash for a farm in the district of Rabbit Hill, Alberta, which he bought from a German, thereby becoming the first Ukrainian settler to have his farm registered in the Land Titles Office in 1896. He was the first Ukrainian to start a settlement south of Edmonton.

The first Ukrainian from Bukovyna said to have come to Canada was Sofroni Mandryk from the village of Shepyntsi, Kitsman County. He emigrated to America in 1894, returned shortly thereafter, sold what he had in Bukovyna, took his family and left for Canada. In 1896 he was the first to homestead in the "Farmalia" district of Alberta, later named Shepenge Post Office and now a railway station called Kayland.

Dr. Oleskiw's trip to Canada in 1895 may have been sponsored by some steamship company, because he did have discussions with the Canadian government while he was here. He intended to open an immigration agency in Galicia. According to the Immigration Act of 10 September 1895, however, the government could not do this, but it did agree to appoint a Ukrainian to the post of immigration officer in Winnipeg. The first was Cyril Genik [Kyrylo Genyk], a close friend of Dr. Oleskiw's, probably from their school days, and it was on Dr. Oleskiw's recommendation that he got the job.

Soon the news spread throughout Galicia and Bukovyna that a Ukrainian, a "Ruthenian," was in charge of immigrants in Canada, and from then on the emigration of Ukrainians from Europe to Canada became a deluge. It assumed such proportions that Dr. Oleskiw was accused of being a traitor—first, by the Austrians because they were losing young Ukrainian boys who made good soldiers for the Austrian army, secondly, by wealthy Polish landowners in the countryside who were losing cheap labour and, thirdly, by Ukrainian patriots who saw emigration as a threat to the nation.

These groups tried to obstruct immigration to Canada in various ways. The Austrian police used force; the gentry and the big landowners frightened the peasants with stories of terrible Canadian winters, worse than in Siberia; others said there was nothing but hunger and misery in Canada. But they could not stop the flood of emigration.

Why Ukrainians Emigrated from Europe to Canada

Long before the establishment of serfdom, Ukraine had fallen under the foreign control of Tatars, Turks, Poles, Russians and a portion was even under the rule of Austro-Hungary. Although from time to time the people rebelled against the invaders, they were unable to free themselves from foreign rule. The invaders worked to impoverish the country and eventually instituted a serfdom that was comparable to the slavery practised by the pharaohs.

With time the upper strata of Ukrainian society was assimilated by the rulers and joined the foreigners in exploiting the poor peasantry and workers through serfdom. In addition, the good Lord sent the Jews who helped the landlord tear the "seventh hide" off the Ukrainian peasant. Eventually the native population was brought to utter ruin.

When serfdom was abolished in Austria in 1848 and in Ukraine under the Russian empire in 1861, freedom of thought, speech and movement began to appear among the pitiful peasants. When they learned that there were countries in the world where there was freedom and plenty of land, they were very interested and did not care where or how far away the countries were so long as they could get away from their Austro-Polish and Russian exploiters. Initially, between 1880 and 1899, it was the young who, one by one, began to flee Austria for America. When, in 1892, Ivan Pillipiw returned from Canada and Dr. Oleskiw's two booklets of 1895 confirmed in print that there were countries across the sea in America where land was given away freely to those who wanted to work it, there was not a power on earth that could hold back those bent on emigration. At first it was primarily those with some income in the Old Country who left for America, thirsting for land and liberty.

For example, from one village, Toporivtsi in Bukovyna, 150 families immigrated to Canada between 1900 and 1910. In those days Cyril Genik in Winnipeg, along with his assistants, H. Havrey, a German from Galicia, and Ivan Puhaty, a Ukrainian from Bukovyna, had to handle the immigration and act as ambassadors of good will. The immigrants from Austro-Hungary and Russia came to them for all kinds of advice and information.

The immigrants helped one another by loaning money to those who had none. This is what Mykhailo Stetsko of Northern Valley, Alberta, had to say about one such incident:

How I Got to Canada

From boyhood I had worked on the estate of a landlord named Khodorovsky in the village of Strilkivtsi, Borshchiv County, Galicia. He was a good man, reasonable and fair. He was a good manager and one felt like working for him. He may have been a Ukrainian, for he spoke the language well.

It was the same on his manor as on the others—the pay was meagre. A man and wife could barely exist on it, and for a larger family poverty was always looking through the window. But this landlord helped people who were deserving.

I was in his service for thirteen years, though not always under his management. When he got older he leased his manor to a Jew named Mendel. The conditions on the estate changed. Mendel cut down on the help and we had to work "overtime," as they say here. But you weren't paid for it the way you are in Canada. You worked from dawn to dusk.

The work got more difficult for me, even though I had been used to hard work from childhood. Mendel wanted us to work like oxen. I was married and we had three children. We had a small cottage and a piece of garden. My father didn't leave me any property when he died because he too had worked all his life at the manor. I didn't get a dowry from my wife either because she also came from a poor family. That's the way it was in the Old Country. A rich girl was ashamed of a stable boy and her parents wouldn't allow her to marry a poor labourer. In Canada it's different.

As the years went by, I often thought about the fate of my children: "As long as we're both healthy and the children are small we'll manage, but what'll happen when they grow up and there are more of them; where'll they end up?" As long as I worked for the landlord, thoughts like that never entered my mind, but once I had to work for Mendel, then for some reason my work didn't interest me, as if something was missing.

One Sunday morning in the spring I made my rounds of the stables and came home for breakfast before my wife and I went to church to pray. I told my wife, Evdokiia—she's dead now, God grant her peace—that I had decided to go to Canada. She stared at me, as if I had gone crazy or gotten sick and was talking in a delirious fever. She asked right away:

"And have you got the money?"

"No, I haven't," I replied, "but I'll borrow it from someone."

"What kind of collateral can you give anyone?"

"I'll borrow on my word of honour," I answered.

"Oh sure, you think someone needs your honour!"

She said this with such vehemence that a tear rolled down her cheek and she quickly wiped it off with her apron.

I didn't say anymore about Canada. The baby in the cradle started to cry and my wife went to look after it, while I went to wash because we were going to church. As soon as we came home from church and had dinner, I left for the manor house. I didn't tell my wife that I was going to the old landlord's.

It was a beautiful day. I remember it as clearly as if it was today. The sun was shining so brightly that my spirit rejoiced. Everything was so spring-like.

The landlord was sitting on the veranda, smoking a long-stemmed pipe. He looked surprised that I had come to see him—on a holiday at that. I approached him, took off my hat, bowed low and said, "Glory to Jesus Christ." I walked up to him and kissed his hand. That was the custom. Peasants kissed the hand of the landlord and the priest. And before I had a chance to tell him why I had come, he asked:

"And what have you to say, Mykhailo?"

"I came to tell you, sir, that I want to emigrate to Canada."

"And what's that got to do with me?" he asked sharply, surprised.

Before I could think of what to say next, he asked, "Is it so bad working on my manor?"

"It's not bad," I said, "but it's not good either. As long as you were in charge, sir, I felt like working, but since you've leased the manor to Mendel the work doesn't come easy."

The landlord immediately left his chair and began pacing the veranda without saying a word. He then stopped and looked out on the lawn bordered with flowers, which the gardener had raised in the rich soil of the hothouse and planted early in the spring.

Whether I offended him or whether he felt sorry, I don't know. He poked the tobacco in his pipe with a tamper to get more smoke, took a few good puffs, turned toward me and asked again, "You're tired of serving on my manor, eh Mykhailo?"

"No, I'm not tired of it, sir, and if I worked for you alone, I'd work and stay on the estate till death, but to work for Mendel—honest to God, I can't. I want to go to Canada and be my own master there. "

"And do you have the money for the trip?" he asked briskly.

"No, I don't. That's why I came to you, sir, to borrow a hundred," I answered.

"What assurance can you give that you'll pay it back?"

"I give you my word of honour that I'll pay it back, sir. And if I, God forbid, should get sick, I'll tell my children to repay it after my death."

He paced the veranda again, thought for a while, then said, "I believe you, Mykhailo. I've always considered you to be an honest worker." He then went inside, leaving me without saying another word.

I was confused and stood there thinking, "Why didn't he tell me if he's going to loan me the money or not?" I stood like that for more than fifteen minutes, my legs beginning to bend at the knees. It seemed to me that I had waited for two hours without the landlord returning. I thought of going, because it seemed he had left me so that I'd leave the manor house all the sooner and return to where I had come from. Luckily, the door swung open and out he came holding a piece of paper in his hand, which he gave to me saying:

"Here, take this paper, go to Borshchiv tomorrow and there at the bank they'll give you a hundred crowns. Go in health to Canada and if things do not work out, return to the village because there'll always be a job for you on my manor."

Ecstatic, I forgot where I was. I embraced the landlord's knees and then kissed both his hands, thanking him the best I knew how. I don't remember how I got home, whether I walked or ran. All I remember is that when I got to the house I was so out of breath that my wife thought someone had been chasing me. Without waiting for her question, I said, "You see, I got the money" Surprised, she asked curiously, "From whom?"

"Why from the landlord," I answered.

"Where is it? Show me."

I quickly reached into my pocket and pulled out the piece of paper landlord Khodorovsky had given me for which I was to get the money and said, "Here it is."

She took the piece of paper into her hands, examined both sides the way a buyer examines a cow at the market, then looked at me and burst out laughing so hard that she started to cry.

"Well, Mykhailo," she said, "I never thought you were that naive. The landlord couldn't get Stetsko out of his parlour, so he gave him a piece of paper to get him out faster." And she started to make even more fun of me and laughed harder.

When I finally pulled myself together, I said to my wife, "Our old landlord never fooled anyone and I don't think he's making a fool of me, because he told me to go to Borshchiv tomorrow and take it to the bank where they would give me a hundred crowns."

When I told her this, she laughed so hard that she had to hold her sides from splitting. I was very embarrassed. I thought perhaps my wife was right, after all, but I wouldn't let on that I had any doubts about what the landlord had done.

The next day, very early in the morning, I made my rounds of the stables, fed the four horses I was in charge of and then went into the village and found a man to take my place at work. I notified Mendel that I was going to Borshchiv and that he should find someone else to take my place the first of the month. He wasn't too pleased with this, but I didn't care and quickly headed for Borshchiv.

In Borshchiv I found the bank, walked in and handed the note from landlord Khodorovsky. The cashier looked it over, verified the landlord's signature and told me to sign on the reverse side. I blushed and told him that I couldn't write. He then called another clerk who signed my name and told me to make a cross. This was the first time in my life that I signed my name with a cross and the first time in my thirty-one years that I owned a hundred crowns. In Canada I've made many crosses and since then have learned what a cheque is.

The cashier counted out a hundred crowns in paper money; I wanted it that way so I wouldn't have trouble with change on the trip. I counted the money myself to be sure the cashier hadn't made a mistake, rolled it up, tied it in a handkerchief, put it inside my shirt and took off for the shortcut between Borshchiv and Strilkivtsi.

When I got home it was already past noon and my wife was waiting impatiently with dinner. I was still outside the doorway when she called out, "Well, is there any money?" I quickly took the bundle out of my shirt and handed it to her saying, "So now will you finally believe that the landlord isn't joking?"

She took the bundle and began to untie the handkerchief

suspiciously. She put the money on the table, folded her hands as if she were praying and exclaimed, "Oh Lord," and quickly ran to the kitchen to get my meal.

In a minute she was back with a bowl of borshch, bread and the second course. She asked me to begin eating by saying, "You must be hungry. Eat while I count the money to see how much you got out of the landlord."

"Didn't I say a hundred crowns."

Two weeks from the day I brought the money from Borshchiv I was already in Hamburg. Other people from our neighbourhood were on their way to Canada, too. It could have been in June but I don't remember for sure, though I do remember it was in 1906. I'm seventy-five and my memory is failing.

I arrived in Canada in the summer and hired out to a farmer for thirty-five dollars per month. I remember that it was very hard to get a job that year, but I was lucky that I didn't have to wander around too long looking for work. It was good for me at that farmer's. I was used to horses from childhood and I wasn't afraid of hard work. He was satisfied with me, too. A German from Russia worked there also and that was very good because he gave me directions in Russian as to what I had to do. The food was good. I never had anything like it in the Old Country. The only problem I had was that I didn't understand the language. I worked there till late fall.

As soon as I got my first month's pay, I sent it immediately to my wife in the Old Country for her support, because Mendel had stopped paying her. She lived on what she could earn from various people and also had three children to feed.

After the harvest the farmer paid me what he owed and I went to Edmonton, but the German remained all winter. He was hired by the year, while I was hired only by the month. From Edmonton I started out for Beaver Creek and then to Beaver Lake, because our people were there already. From them I wanted to learn where there were good homesteads so I could pick one for myself, which is why I had come to Canada. The good people directed me all the way to Myrnam, where there were still farms for the taking. I chose one in the forest north of Landonville, Alberta. The post office there is now named Northern Valley. It's south of Elk Point. During that winter I built a house in which I spent almost the whole winter alone. There was no one else there at the time. I was the first, and the nearest post office was Landonville. It was forty-five miles to Vermilion through the bush and there weren't any roads.

In the spring I got a job on a railroad section gang right in Vermilion, and the money I earned I sent to my wife for steamship tickets. She also sold the house and garden and with the children came to Alberta. This was in the fall. I led her through the dark forest to the house which I had built myself. This was the first structure I had ever put up in my life. They say that "necessity is the mother of invention." That's the way many of our peasants, who didn't even know how to make a tooth for a rake in the Old Country, became architects in Canada.

On the farm we worked like CNR mules. The trees were so thick you couldn't see the sun through them. Moose, elk and deer roamed everywhere. Now it's the nicest district in Alberta. Although I worked very hard, I'm not sorry. I like this district very much. I'm satisfied with my work. I'm seventy-five years old and I live with my son. I'm proud of my healthy grandchildren, who are having an easier time of it than my children. All our children had to work hard. While my wife and I cleared the land, the poor little ones dragged and burned the branches and tree stumps. Only their white teeth shone. But, thank God, we had ten of them and all were healthy. It's true we lost two to the flu in 1918, but in those days more of the healthy children died than the sickly ones. I now get the old age pension. God grant good health to the one who brought that about. A man shouldn't have to look to anyone for charity. There are always some new pennies for good old tobacco. Without tobacco I don't know if I could live, that's how much I like to smoke. I still have a strong chest and I also had a strong mother. Take my own children and grandchildren—they're all as solid as cucumbers. Oh yes, health's the greatest treasure on earth. He who hasn't good health is a poor man.

Some might think that our people grew up in the lap of luxury, but speaking for myself, I worked very hard in the Old Country and I didn't spend my time fiddling with a pen or pencil in Canada. My children were fed simple food and were raised without any comforts. Thank God, they grew up like oak trees.

But I haven't told you the story of how I returned the money to my good landlord in Strilkivtsi. It took five years from the time I left the Old Country for Canada. That fifth year I made some money on the railroad, sold two young steers and sent every last penny with interest in a money order to landlord Khodorovsky. I thanked him for his gracious patience and good will and wrote him a letter describing my life and my farm in Canada. I don't know whether he believed me, but I wrote that I had 160 acres with enough forest to heat all of Galicia; that fifteen acres were under cultivation; that I had two oxen, a cow, a wagon, plough, harrow and sleigh, a house and five children, two of whom had been born in Canada. I thought it might please him that he had loaned money to Stetsko on trust. He was a good landlord and that's why I speak well of him. Oh, he's dead now. I tell my children that there are good people in this world, too. That man was no ordinary type but an aristocrat among aristocrats and a good manager. May God grant him heavenly peace.

Mykhailo Stetsko's recollections were gathered and written down by W. A. Czumer and W. S. Plawiuk [Plaviuk] in the Stetsko home in Northern Valley, Alberta, on 31 May 1941.

~3~

What the Ukrainians Brought with Them to Canada

Any Ukrainian peasant who owned something of value in the Old Country would sell it and with the money would buy steamship tickets for himself and his family. Whatever remained was kept for living expenses in Canada. Those who had more property, such as a house, garden, land and livestock, also sold it and tried to bring agricultural implements with them, thinking they would be of use here. However, as soon as they were convinced by those already in Canada that such implements were not suited for cultivating the soil, they stopped bringing them.

Other items such as the spade, hoe, saw, axe, scythe, sickle, rake, flail, hammer, wood auger, hay fork, stable fork, etc., were packed in large crates and taken along. Some also brought a handmill [*zhorna*] for grinding grain, while others brought a mortar [*stupa*] for grinding barley into groats for porridge. The poor colonists found the handmill, in particular, to be very useful. With it they ground wheat into flour for baking brown bread. Some also brought looms for weaving hemp and broadcloth. What survived the longest among the settlers were the looms for weaving tapestries, coverlets, sashes and towels. The Ukrainians also brought their village dress and kitchen utensils and used them for a long time, until they wore out.

Although not very stylish, the village clothing from the Old Country lasted a long time because it was made from linen or hemp cloth, while winter clothes were made of broadcloth and sheepskin. The English called these sheepskin coats "Galician sheepskins." Although similar coats were manufactured in America, they were of sheared wool and covered with waterproof cloth or broadcloth. When their village clothes wore out, Ukrainians became the major purchasers of American sheepskin coats and wool jackets called mackinaws and linen jackets and overalls in the summer.

The people who retained their national dress in Canada the longest were the elderly Ukrainian women. As late as the celebrations of the fiftieth anniversary of Ukrainian immigration to Canada, one could still meet in various settlements elderly women dressed in their national costume—white silk or flowered kerchief-shawls covering their heads, white linen blouses, cloth or fur vests [*kiptaryk* or *katsabayka*], black cloth skirts [*horbatka*] and knee-high yellow boots of goatskin or else Canadian-made yellow shoes.

At first, as soon as young Ukrainian people became Canadianized, they felt ashamed of their national dress. But when it began to disappear, they tried to revive it by wearing it proudly on national holidays and in theatrical performances. They had modernized the dress so much that even other nationalities began to take an interest in it. A store specializing in Ukrainian women's embroidered blouses, skirts and jackets would do quite well because people like new styles and Ukrainian dress is easy to introduce in Canada.

What Ukrainian Pioneers Found in Canada: Their First Impressions

Before setting out for Canada, the average Ukrainian peasant had read or heard about the wealth of America, so in his mind it represented "God's Paradise" on earth. Caught up in the vision, he set out with high hopes. However, once he had left behind the borders of his native land, had suffered seasickness on the way over, had travelled through western Ontario's rocky cliffs, lakes, swamps, forests and muskeg until the train had rocked him past endurance, and had had to deal with strangers who only spoke a foreign language, and in the West had been greeted by freezing winds and all kinds of adventures and discomforts on the way, then his once rosy dream of Canada as "God's Paradise" quickly disappeared. He felt disillusioned and almost broken in spirit. There were, in addition, all kinds of misadventures, similar to that related by Georgii Martyniuk of Shandro, Alberta:

An Incident Between Ukrainian Settlers on Their Way to Alberta and Railway Officials on the Saskatchewan Prairie

It was late in the spring of 1899 when a big trainload of Ukrainian immigrants arrived in Winnipeg. Some got off the train, while eighty families from Bukovyna and half of those from Galicia set off to go further west, all the way to Alberta. In Hamburg we Bukovynians had paid the fare to Alberta because our people had already settled on farms there, and so that was where we also wanted to go. Of those from Galicia, however, some had paid their fares to Assiniboia, while others only to Winnipeg. The latter remained on the train, having decided while still aboard ship to stick with us Bukovynians and go right to Alberta, since they didn't know anyone else in Canada nor where to look for homesteads. Our train stayed in Winnipeg for over an hour and then headed west.

The next day, around noon, our train stopped in the middle of the wide, empty prairie. Curious, we poked our heads out the windows to get a good look and to see the name of the station. But there was no station, only a small shed painted red, with not a soul in sight either by the shed or on the prairie. All around us were the empty, boundless plains covered with gophers, animals we had never seen in the Old Country.

Looking at the prairie, we were surprised that, even though the land looked good for cultivation, for some reason there wasn't even a twig of a tree growing on it and nobody lived there. While wondering why such good land lay wasted and unsettled, shouts and cries from women and children came from the second car in front of us. We thought there was an accident or that someone had died or fallen sick, causing the conductors to stop the train. Leaning out of the windows, we turned in the direction of the cries and the wailing and saw people coming out of the cars with luggage in their hands. They were extremely upset, as if someone was forcibly throwing them out onto the prairie. They were crying.

Before we could understand what was happening, the door of our car swung open and in came a railway official and an immigration agent in his official cap and brass buttons, looking like a tax collector or officer from the Old Country. The agent had only one arm. They said he was Genik because he spoke Ukrainian, but later we found out that it wasn't Genik but Havrey, a German from Stryi in Galicia. In Canada he was in charge of settling immigrants on farms. We Bukovynians, on our way to Alberta, were surprised by this unexpected event. We asked the armless agent why we were being ordered off the train, and he said,

"This is Assiniboia where you're supposed to look for your farms."
We began to argue that we knew nothing of any "Siniboia." We were going to Alberta and we refused to leave our cars. He then got as stern with us as an Old Country policeman and told us that we had to get out. The railway officials joined in to help him and began demanding that we get out, but we couldn't understand them.

Together we Bukovynians surrounded the armless one and began to attack him, accusing him of betrayal and of wishing to dump us in this wasteland to perish in a foreign land. But he kept insisting that this "Siniboia" was the place where we had to settle.

The behaviour of the armless agent shocked and infuriated us. How could we get off the train in the middle of nowhere with our children and families, when there wasn't a house or even a tent in which to spend the night? "Who ever heard of such a thing," we said.

The conductor understood that something was wrong because we firmly held our ground insisting that they must take us to Alberta or else back to Winnipeg, to our man Genik, who had written us that things were good in Canada, that he'd take care of our people, that no one would come to any harm and that one could take land wherever one wished. Yet here we were being ordered off the train to settle in this desert. We were asked to show our tickets. They were in good order: we had paid from Hamburg all the way to Edmonton. Then they began talking among themselves and went down to the locomotive, where they talked some more. Finally, they uncoupled the locomotive from our cars and took off leaving us on the prairie.

Those who had been first to leave their cars got back in, and we told them that God forbid that anyone should dare get off and be left behind in this wilderness. When the agent and the railroad officials took off in the engine, probably to the nearest town to telegraph, we reflected on our stubborn immigrant-Bukovynian refusal to settle on the prairies of "Siniboia." We got out of the cars and sat in a circle like Indians on the prairie and began to hold a council on what all this meant.

The women, too, came out, sobbing and reproaching their husbands for needlessly wanting to come to Canada. "Now do you see," they said, "here's Canada for you."

I told them not to worry, that everything would be all right, that it wasn't as bad as all that. So they uncoupled the engine and took off. So what? Let them go. We ought to be glad they left us the cars. And I assured them that they'd take us where they're supposed to.

We sat on the prairie for more than five hours. Some cried and moaned that they had come to a foreign land to perish; others laughed and joked saying, "The road to hell is easy, but that to heaven is hard."

The sun was already setting far in the west, but there was no sign of the gentlemen in the locomotive. We thought we'd have to spend the night on the prairie. The women began to feed the children and to divy up the food for supper. The children ran around without a care chasing gophers, which were themselves ready for sleep because they "peeped" like chicks before a rain. The children had fun because they had never seen such animals before, but for us adults the time dragged on.

While we waited we talked about everything. Some said this was some sort of deceit because the advertisements had praised Canada, when in reality it wasn't at all the way it was made out to be. Others said it was a mistake caused by those who had tickets for "Siniboia." Others thought that here was uninhabited prairie which they wanted to fill up with Galicians, but there wasn't even anything with which to put a hut together. The only thing to do would be to dig a hole in the ground, clawing like a bear and living in it like an animal. Anyway, we slandered Canada from head to toe. Nevertheless, I stood by my conviction that Alberta wasn't "Siniboia." Our people from Banyliv had written that in Alberta there was both forest and good land, but they never mentioned any "Siniboia."

Late in the evening our gentlemen returned with the locomotive. They quickly came to us and began speaking gently. "There was a mistake," they said. "This train isn't going to Alberta and those with tickets to Assiniboia will be let off at the nearest station. This train will stay there overnight. In the morning a freight train bound for Alberta will arrive and take those who are going there."

That's what happened. Very early the next morning the train came, our cars were hitched behind it and we were taken all the way to Edmonton. In Alberta we already felt at home. Here we met our own people and found a nice countryside, not a treeless waste like "Siniboia."

We disembarked at Strathcona, which is now South Edmonton, and stopped overnight at the Immigration Hall. On the third day we went out to look for farms. We searched for two weeks and finally found good land in a place now called Sunland.

Once in Edmonton, we joked with the Galicians saying, "Hey, if it wasn't for us stubborn Bukovynians you'd be eating gophers in 'Siniboia'." And they'd respond, "That's why we stuck with you Hutsuls,* because Hutsuls know where are the woods and meadows."

The First Ukrainian Settlements in Canada

Few of us had made any effort previously to find out where and when and by whom the first Ukrainian settlements were begun in Western Canada. Almost no one was interested in the question. Even today, it is difficult to say who was the first in a district that

---

* Ukrainians from the Carpathian Mountains. (Ed.)

is now almost totally Ukrainian. We have only the stories told by
the old pioneers themselves.

In Manitoba. Ukrainian families had come to Manitoba from
Galicia in 1892, but they had not formed colonies in the
countryside. The first peasants, Ivan Pillipiw and Wasyl Eleniak
from Nebyliv in Kalush County, had arrived in 1891 as labourers,
not settlers. The next year seven families from that village arrived
in Canada. They were the families of Vasyl Iatsiv, Mykhailo
Romaniuk, M. Eleniak, Ios. [Iosyf] Paish, A. Paish, Nykola
Tychkovsky and D. Vyzhynovych. Except for A. Paish and
N. Tychkovsky, who left this group for another on its way to
Alberta, they all remained in Winnipeg. Some found jobs in the
city; others went to work for German Mennonites from Russia at
Gretna in southern Manitoba. But in a few years, all except Vasyl
Iatsiv could be found on farms in the Beaver Creek and Beaver
Lake districts of Alberta.

The first real colony of Ukrainians in Manitoba started in 1896
near Stuartburn. That same year there were settlements at Gonor
and Brokenhead further east, and in the Dauphin area, northwest of
Winnipeg. The following families resided in the Stuartburn district:
Prybizhansky, Podolsky, Pryhorsky, Zaharia, Shtefura, Kishchuk,
Stefanovych, Smuk, Kohut, Dumansky and many others from
Galicia and Bukovyna.

By 1897 and 1898 the number of Ukrainian colonies in Manitoba
had increased substantially. They existed at Sifton, Ethelbert, Pine
River, Gilbert Plains, Duck Mountain and Rocky Mountain,
Sandilands, Menzie, Rossburn, Strathclair, Shoal Lake, Teulon,
Pleasant Home, Gimli and others.

In Saskatchewan. In Saskatchewan the first Ukrainian colony
appeared in 1896 in the Grenfell district, but it quickly disappeared
because the people left, probably because there was no forest.
Ukrainians preferred wooded areas which provided fuel and
materials for building. The following year, there was a rapid growth
of Ukrainian colonies in the northern part of the province, in the
Duck Lake, Fish Creek and Crooked Lake districts, where now
there are the towns of Wakaw, St. Julien and Rosthern. The following settlers were there at the time: Romanchych, Malkovych,
Zalieshchuk, Mykhailiuk, Bodnarchuk, Bilinsky and numerous
others. They all most likely came from eastern Galician Austria.

In Alberta. In 1892 Nykolai Tychkovsky and A. Paish were the first Ukrainians to settle on farms in Alberta, among German colonists in the Bruderheim district. In 1893 Ivan Pillipiw and probably Stefan Chichak joined them. The next year the people of Nebyliv established a settlement in the valley of Beaver Creek, which flows into Beaver Lake. Among them were the families of Ivan Pillipiw, Vasyl Feniak, Pullishy, Paish, Eleniak, Dobrutsky, five families of Melnyks and still others. Later the colony expanded far to the south into the Beaver Lake district and to the north across the North Saskatchewan River to Victoria. Today it is the largest settlement in Western Canada, over a hundred miles long and seventy miles wide.

By 1896 Ukrainian settlers were coming to Alberta from Western Galicia and from Bukovyna. Some from Western Galicia settled at Brudherheim, while others chose Rabbit Hill, south of Edmonton. Although there were Germans, Hungarians, Swedes and others already there, the Ukrainians wedged themselves in and began buying land from the earlier colonists. Today the population of Rabbit Hill district is 70 per cent Ukrainian. The Rabbit Hill settlement was started by Fedko Fuhr from the village of Bysotko, Iaroslav County in Western Galicia. He bought his farm from a German for cash and so became the first Ukrainian landowner in Canada. In 1896 he already held legal title to his land. In 1898 the following had joined him in Rabbit Hill: Dobko, Pidhirny, Olekshy [Olekshii], Sereda, Borys, Workun [Vorkun], Pyrch, Manchak, Khimera, Fytsovych and many others.

The first Ukrainian from Bukovyna who farmed in Alberta was Sofroni Mandryk from the village of Shepyntsi in Kitsman County. He started the Shepenge colony, now Kayland, Alberta. In 1894 he left his village for the U.S. After two years he returned to Bukovyna, took his family and went to ⌐anada. After him, both poor and well-off Ukrainians emigrated en masse from Bukovyna. Some settled in Stuartburn, Manitoba, but most settled in the Egg Lake district of Alberta. They called it "Iglick" in their own idiom. It is now called the Andrew district and the post office is named Whitford. Others settled on unsurveyed land in the Victoria district, where there was a Hudson's Bay trading post on the North Saskatchewan and the post office is named Pakan. This is probably the most populous and extensive colony of Bukovynians in Western Canada.

The Difficult Fate of Early Ukrainian Colonists in Canada

It is difficult to describe the hard times faced by the early Ukrainian settlers in this new country. We have only bits and pieces told by the pioneers themselves. Kost Zaharichuk [Zahariichuk] of Smoky Lake, Alberta, tells the following story:

> I came to Canada in 1898 from the village of Toporivtsi in Bukovyna. I came with the family and we stayed with half-breeds at Pakan, Alberta. We were poor. We had only ten dollars cash when we arrived in Pakan, eighty miles east of Edmonton. It was fall and I decided to go on to Fort Saskatchewan to find work with some farmer. There a German hired me to dig potatoes and in a week I earned ten sacks. It was the greatest stroke of luck because it meant we wouldn't starve that winter. When I wrote my wife that I had earned ten sacks of potatoes, she couldn't believe it and came fifty miles on foot to see for herself if it was really true. As the German was to deliver the potatoes after threshing, I buried them in the ground so they wouldn't freeze. In exchange for his delivering the potatoes all the way to Pakan, I had to clay plaster his barn so the cattle would be warm.
>
> My wife couldn't wait. She came on foot and took almost a full sack to Pakan, carrying it the fifty miles on her back. Then she came back two more times to see that the potatoes hadn't frozen or been stolen. Both times she tried to put a sack on her shoulders to carry back to Pakan, but the German woman wouldn't let her.
>
> "You're a stupid woman," she said. "Someday you'll pay dearly for this with your health. If my husband said he'd deliver your potatoes he'll deliver them."
>
> I continued to work on the threshing machine and when the snow came the German took my potatoes and me home. My wife knelt over those potatoes and prayed for an hour. She thanked God for not letting us starve to death in Canada. In the spring when our people found out I had potatoes for seeding, they came from as far away as twenty miles to ask for them. We gave some to everyone, and do you know what they did? They cut out the potato eyes to use for planting and from the centre they made soup to feed the small children, because there wasn't any milk. Tell people nowadays about those hardships and they wouldn't believe you, but I'll remember them as long as I live.
>
> Early in the spring of 1899, I chose a piece of land ten miles north of Pakan, where the town of Smoky Lake now stands. Although the land wasn't surveyed, I still wanted a place to build a hut for my family while I went to look for work. It took my wife and me a whole week to carry our things on our backs through the bush from Pakan to our homestead. The worst thing was carrying our Old Country trunk through the bush and fallen trees, but it contained all our belongings.

There was no road to the place, so you couldn't get there by wagon. I was the first homesteader there. Today you can still see the house that my wife and little ten-year-old son, Petro, built. That spring I put up just a shelter so they could get out of the rain and sleep peacefully at night without worrying about wild animals. There were all kinds there, mostly moose, coyotes and bears.

As soon as we had moved our "treasures" to the homestead, I took off on foot for Edmonton, eighty miles away, and left my wife and children in the bush. I left them a sack of "4X Flour," some potatoes and a piece of salt pork to live on, but not a penny in cash. The only five dollars we had I took because without money a man could perish on the road.

There was a Hudson's Bay store at Pakan, where Indians and half-breeds traded. I asked Mitchell, the manager, to give my wife sugar, corn meal and salt pork if she came to get them and as soon as I had a job I'd send him money. I don't know how I explained it all to him, but he said, "All right, Kost."

There was no work in Edmonton. I was there for three days and on the fourth I got a job splitting wood at a hotel. For that I got dinner, a loaf of bread and forty cents. The next day I bought two more loaves of bread and some smoked pork and started walking down the railroad track to Calgary, where I thought I'd find work sooner because it was bigger and older. Along the way I stopped to ask farmers for work. On the fourth day I got to Red Deer, more than a hundred miles from Edmonton. Whenever night fell, I slept in someone's barn or even in a haystack or a pile of straw.

In Red Deer I came across some Germans from Russia who told me to go to Gleichen, where the farmers were well-established and better off. There was a good chance of getting work there. I got a job at a German's twenty miles north of "Galician," which is the way our people pronounced the name. The Germans pronounced it "Glaiken" and the English "Glayshen." We Ukrainians said "Galician" because it was easier to pronounce that way.

I worked there all summer and made forty dollars cash, and on top of that the farmer gave me a mare in foal and a cow. I can't tell you or explain how much I treasured those animals. A rich man likely doesn't appreciate his millions or enjoy his own children as much as I cherished those earnings. I tied a rope to the animals and led them on foot all the way to Wetaskiwin.

It took me four days and three nights to reach Wetaskiwin because I had to let them graze. I went to a farm to ask for something to eat, because the food I had been given by the lady of the house at the place where I had worked was all gone and I felt weak. The farmer, who saw me leading the animals while I was barely able to stand up, asked me how far I had led them and where I was taking them. I told him and he said, "You're crazy! You've got a horse and you're walking! Tie the cow to the horse's tail, get on the horse and ride like a man." So I did. I rode home on horseback from Wetaskiwin. I could have done this from the start but I felt sorry for the horse in foal.

When I brought the animals to the homestead my wife panicked. She thought I had probably driven up somebody else's livestock and she started to harangue me. I had to convince her that I had earned them. My wife may have been taken aback by the animals, but I was equally surprised at the new place she and the boy had built during the summer. She had plastered it inside and out with clay and thatched the roof with reeds, which she had cut at a nearby lake and carried a half-mile to the house. In the house there was a new baby in a cradle made from Canadian willow. When I left to look for a job in the spring none of this existed. And that's how we began to prosper in Canada.

How We Floated on a Raft from Edmonton to Our Homestead: The Story of Mariia Eurchuk [Iuriichuk] of Hamlin, Alberta

It was the end of September 1899 when seven families, five from Bukovyna and our two from Galicia, arrived in Edmonton. The Bukovynians had friends in Alberta and on the third day they chanced on transportation going to "Iglick" [Egg Lake], which is now the district of Andrew. They paid fifteen dollars per family and we'd have gone, too, but we had only $7.50 to our name. Although we needed it for supplies, we'd have gladly parted with our last cent. The driver, however, wanted fifteen dollars, which we didn't have.

Our husbands decided to look for homesteads a little closer to Edmonton. For a whole week they tramped around hungry and on foot looking in forest, sand and swamp for homesteads, but they couldn't find any good land because it had been taken up long ago and you had to go perhaps a hundred miles from Edmonton, away to the east or to the north, to get anything worthwhile. A man looking for a homestead with my husband—I've forgotten his name now—met an acquaintance on some sandy land and went there with his family. I was left alone with my little children in the Immigration Hall in Strathcona. As long as others were there I wasn't so lonely, but when my friend left and my husband was out all day in town looking for anyone at all to take us to Pasichny's* in Victoria (whose address we had), I'd be by myself with the children and would feel so alone that my heart felt like it would break from grief. I'd cry. The children cried. I thought I'd go insane from despair. Nobody would take us to Victoria. They wanted twenty dollars which we didn't have, nor was there any use staying in Strathcona because winter was coming and we had no money to live on.

---

* Quite likely Pasichnek as there were no Pasichnys settled south of Victoria in the Shandro area. (Ed.)

Finally, my husband decided to put a raft together and float down the river, 120 miles east to Pasichny's, who lived at Victoria on the bank of the North Saskatchewan. His post office address was Whitford.

My husband was healthy and strong, but not a very smart Hutsul. Those who lived in the Carpathians were called Hutsuls. My husband worked in the forest cutting trees and floating them by raft down the Cheremosh River, all the way to Moldavia. In Bukovyna he heard that people were going to Canada and on the spur of the moment decided to go as well, without realizing that it was no big matter getting there but once there the problem was survival. Our Hutsuls used to have a saying, "If you don't know the ford, don't go into the water," but my husband didn't understand that. He was quick to take anybody's advice, and because of this he and I have suffered throughout our lives. As if it wasn't enough that we had slaved clearing bush in Alberta, in his old age he decided to go to British Columbia to have us dig huge cedar stumps. He died there and there I also lost my only son, who drowned in the river floating logs at a sawmill.

But I didn't finish telling you how we used the raft to get to Pasichny's in Victoria. As soon as my husband built the raft on the river at Strathcona, we began moving our things from the hostel (where I had been for two weeks) to the raft. Things went so-so until it came to moving the trunk, which contained all we owned. It weighed about four hundred pounds. People gathered and laughed at us as if we were fools. My husband couldn't speak English and he didn't know enough to ask for a drayman to help take it to the raft. Finally, one came along, saw the trouble we were having rolling the trunk down the street, pulled up and told us to put it on the dray. My husband walked ahead of the horses to show the way. And when he got to the river the drayman burst out laughing. The local children came running, curious to see how we would float. Everyone was laughing and yelling, "Galicians go homestead."

The drayman wouldn't take any money. He just waved his hand and said, "Bye-bye." It was already afternoon when we pushed off from the bank onto the river. The next day, toward evening, we were near the ferry at Fort Saskatchewan, which is twenty-five miles east of Edmonton.

The water in the river was low and the raft drifted along very slowly. We came across Russian-speaking Germans who told us it would take a whole week to reach far-away Victoria. We only had enough food to last two days, so my husband had to run to the Fort to buy potatoes, pork fat and bread. On the raft we had a sheet of tin on which we made a fire, roasted potatoes and smeared them with pork fat, and that's how we ate.

My husband also built a shanty on the raft for shelter from wind and rain and that's where our children slept at night. We travelled by raft at night. One of us would try to get some sleep while the other watched that the raft didn't drift into shallow water or hit the bank and get wrecked.

The raft drifted along very slowly and on the third night, when a very heavy snow began to fall, we wrapped ourselves in blankets and sat hunched up in the shanty, not noticing how our raft was being carried to a sand bar in shallow water, where it stopped. We went barefoot into the water to push the raft, but try as we might it wouldn't budge, and there we spent the whole night. The snow fell heavily, as if determined to bury us alive. It was impossible to build a fire because the firewood my husband had gathered in Edmonton got wet and wouldn't burn. We thought morning would see the end of us. We were so cold our teeth rattled. I cried over my fate and cursed my husband and his Canada. Around noon the next day some Indians who lived near the river bank noticed us and came to see what was on the sand bar. They took us to some old cabin, made some hot tea, gave us some dry bannock and we finally revived. Our children were not as frozen as my husband and I. They had slept through the night because I had covered them with a quilt which we had brought with us from the Old Country. But we caught very bad colds because we had gone into the water to free the raft. I won't forget it as long as I live.

Think about it! There we were on the river, in mud, surrounded by water with snow falling like crazy—nothing but wilderness, not knowing where we were, how far we still had to go or where to look for people to help us get the raft afloat. It was a godsend that the Indians noticed us and came out of curiosity. If it wasn't for them, we'd have perished.

We were rescued by the Indians with a canoe, which they probably used to cross the river. They took everything [off the raft] easily except for that trunk of ours, which caused problems again.

When we'd warmed up a bit, the Indians tried to talk to us, but we couldn't understand them at all. In Edmonton my husband had been taught to say three words of English, "Me go homestead, Pasichny, Victoria," and that is what he kept saying to the Indians. They must have understood because they asked, "You Galician?" My husband didn't know what this word meant but he nodded his head yes. They took him outside and pointed to a path over the hill and told him to follow it to Stefan Ratsoy's, "a Galician." It was a ten-mile walk because the Indians showed us the fingers of both hands. My husband understood them and walked all the way to Pakan, where half-breeds directed him to Ratsoy's, who had already lived there for two years with his own horses. Meanwhile, my children and I remained with the Indians. They too had children who tried to talk to mine, but they couldn't understand each other.

Toward evening Stefan Ratsoy came in a wagon and my husband placed all our things in it. The raft with the shanty on it remained at

Pine Creek. The next morning Ratsoy took us twenty-five miles to Pasichny's, where the post office is now called Wasel.

You couldn't list on an ox's hide all the miseries I have experienced in Canada. It wasn't enough that for twenty-two years we pulled stumps in Alberta, but my husband got it into his head to go to British Columbia to dig cedar stumps for fifteen years. That's where he died and I lost my only son. He was pushing logs into the river at the sawmill and fell into the water and drowned under the logs. I returned to Alberta. I'm getting my old age pension now and living with my daughter, who is married to Petro Luchak of Hamlin, Alberta. But when I think of my native country and my youth, my heart almost breaks with sorrow. It was joyful to live there, but here I worked so hard and had no luck. Maybe Canada is a good country, but not for me.

What It Was Like for Ukrainians to Leave Their Native Village for Canada

When the peoples of Western Europe were emigrating to America, they had emigration societies which were concerned with their problems and helped them in whatever way they could. In many cases, church leaders and government authorities in their native country were also involved. The western European immigrant was well-informed about his destination and the situation facing him there.

It was different with the Ukrainians. They did not have their own organizations or societies either in Europe or Canada. The Austro-Hungarian empire, from where the majority of Ukrainians emigrated, did not care what happened to them in Canada, nor did their own Ukrainian church. They were going, as they themselves put it, "At God's will and in the care of the steamship agents."

Those Ukrainians who left to settle in America or Canada were thought to be lost to the homeland and nation. Often in church, when the priest gave his blessing to a departing family or group, not only the relatives but the whole village wept more than at a funeral. The women, crying like little children, kissed each other good-bye saying, "Farewell, sister, we won't see each other till Josaphat's Valley."

How did the simple peasant get all that courage and determination to leave when he knew absolutely nothing about the country to which he was going? Many a peasant said, "Oh well, what will happen, will happen, but it can't be worse than here in Austria." Even so, it was not easy to leave relatives, neighbours, friends and one's native village. One had to be tough not to break down. For a family to leave relatives they would never see again and go to a strange country was worse than death. There were cases of women fainting from sorrow and despair, and of mothers separated from their children, taking some with them to Canada and leaving others behind.

The scene repeated itself in Canada when friends had to separate to go in different directions and to unknown places. Some were lost on the wide prairies; others disappeared in the dark forests. Years went by and they lost track of each other. They were as lost as chicks without a hen. And truly, God must have been with them and their faith in Him gave them strength and perseverance. They remembered the Ukrainian proverb: "Ask God but use your hands" or "God helps those who help themselves." That is what they did. They helped each other as best they could. And though they had little national awareness, their common language and national and religious traditions bound them together. But there was one question they could not resolve: "Why was there a single Ukrainian people but two faiths?"

Longing for Their Homeland and Church

A full five years had passed from the time Ukrainian immigration had begun, and in all that time not one Ukrainian priest, either Catholic or Orthodox, had appeared among the immigrants in Canada.* The people felt forsaken. They saw that other nationalities, including a small group of Poles, had their own priests in Canada. Only the Ukrainians had been forgotten. This bothered them and, even more, made them resentful of their church leaders in the Old Country. They longed for their homeland. When

---

* The Ukrainians who came to Canada were divided into two main religious groups, the Greek Catholics primarily from Galicia and the Greek Orthodox mainly from Bukovyna. The Greek Catholic or Uniate church came into being in 1596 as a result of Roman Catholic missionary efforts after the Union of Lublin in 1569, when the Kingdom of Poland came to control most of Ukraine. The Uniate church was a blend of Roman Catholic dogma and doctrine and the Eastern or Greek rite. (Ed.)

important holidays like Christmas and Easter rolled around, they
met at the home of some individual who had a large house, felt sorry
for themselves and discussed what to do. "What future is there for
us and our church in Canada?" they asked. "Where will our children
get together to celebrate our native customs in this foreign land?"

Both the Orthodox and the Catholic Ukrainians worried about
having their native church in Canada, because they both faced the
same situation. They were not used to being without religion and
they were not satisfied with foreign rites. From the start, the question brought together the Orthodox from Bukovyna and the
Catholics from Galicia. Each longed in the same way for the familiar.

In the *Ukrainskyi holos* of 20 April 1940, Mariia Adamovsky
described those times. Her account is published here in abridged
form:

Easter in My Native Village

Although it was long ago, I can see the lively, fresh scenes of Easter
as clearly as if it were today. I see my native village at the bottom of a
mountain basking in the sun, its cottages white as cherry blossoms and
on a hill, the church. I see my own little cottage and in it my mother,
now deceased, waking me early to wash my face for church so I would
not be late because today is a great and solemn holy day—Easter. The
cherry leaves rustle among the cottages and the fragrance of their
blossoms fills the universe. The entire village resounds with the joyous
chirping of birds, in particular the nightingale and the cuckoo. It is all
so enchanting.

Beside the church I see a great number of people and long rows of
baskets filled with all kinds of God's gifts—eggs, Easter eggs, cheese,
butter, sausage rings, ham, Easter bread—all good things ready to be
blessed. The joyous hymn "Christ Has Risen" fills the air.

After the Easter service people merrily make their way home and the
village grows still for a while. Then, following the old custom, everyone
hurries to the belfry to ring the bells and the young people gather to
play *hayilky* [spring songs and games], nothing being more fun or more
relaxing for a villager than that. By the church a group of girls sings:

Here comes, here comes Zelman
Here comes, here comes his brother
Zelman's mother,

And his sister-in-law
And his whole family.*

In remembering the Easter of my childhood in my native village, I cherish even to this day the memories of those great moments.

This reminiscence is only one reflection of what was felt in the hearts of thousands of pioneers in Western Canada. The loss of religion—their longing for their church and homeland and their native customs and way of life—spurred the pioneers to united action to create familiar surroundings in a foreign land.

Russian Missionaries Among Ukrainians in Canada

Years went by and the settlers had not heard either their own liturgy or divine service. They took it as God's punishment, because neither the Orthodox nor the Catholics were used to a life without religion. When emigrating, they had never given it any thought. The church authorities did not try to provide even a single priest for these unfortunate people. To soothe their conscience somehow, the immigrant pioneers gathered in some person's home for common prayer and often held matins as best they could. They considered this the fulfilment of their religious duties. They did not attend foreign churches because they did not understand the language. And even if sometimes they were visited by a Polish Roman Catholic priest, his rite was far different from the Ukrainian one.** Besides, even in the Old Country the Ukrainians despised Polish priests for some reason and considered them their enemies.

But in July of 1897 two Russian Orthodox missionaries came to Alberta, the priest Romanov and the psalmist Alexandrov.*** At

---

* The beginning of one of the most popular Ukrainian folk songs sung at Easter. The origin of the figure of Zelman is uncertain. In the Ukrainian version he comes with his relatives to seek a bride. (Ed.)

** Ukrainian church ritual was conducted according to the Eastern, Byzantine or Greek rite with the Mass sung in Old Church Slavonic, as distinct from the Western, Roman or Latin rite Mass sung in Latin. (Ed.)

*** Father Dimitri Kameneff and Deacon Vladimir Alexandroff, according to P. Yuzyk, "The Ukrainian Greek Orthodox Church of Canada" (unpublished Ph.D. thesis, University of Minnesota, 1958), 76. (Ed.)

the time, talk at the Beaver Creek colony had it that they had been invited to come to Canada from San Francisco by Messrs. Sakman and Nemirsky, who lived in the district later known as Wostok. They were originally from Galicia. On 6 July 1897 (Julian calendar) these two missionaries celebrated the first Divine Liturgy in the open on the farm of Theodore Nemirsky. The Ukrainian settlers at Beaver Creek were so pleased with the arrival of the two monks that they asked them to come again. From then on, these two Russian missionaries not only returned time and again to Alberta, but also visited colonies in Saskatchewan and Manitoba.

Roman Catholic Bishop Legal Becomes Alarmed

The unexpected appearance of the Russian priests amid Ukrainian Greek Catholic settlers upset Bishop Legal, the Roman Catholic bishop in St. Albert. Bishop Legal was told of the arrival of the "schismatics" (the name bestowed on the Orthodox by the Catholics) by Reverend Olszewski, who lived in the Beaver Creek district in what is now the town of Hilliard. He served both the Roman Catholic and the Ukrainian Catholic communities.

The arrival of the Russian missionaries disturbed Bishop Legal because they came to his diocese and he had been empowered by the Roman Catholic hierarchy to care for Ukrainian Greek Catholics in Alberta. Soon afterward, Bishop Legal, quite likely with the co-operation of Archbishop Langevin of Winnipeg, brought the Reverend Nestor Dmytriw [Dmytriv], a Ukrainian Greek Catholic priest, to Canada from the United States for the first time.

Reverend Dmytriw held his first service among the Greek Catholic settlers of Stuartburn, Manitoba, and then visited Alberta in the fall. He arrived at Beaver Creek along with Bishop Legal and held the first Ukrainian Greek Catholic Mass in the Old Church Slavonic language in the Limestone Lake School.

Bishop Legal did not participate in the Ukrainian service; he only looked on, probably because it was the first time he had ever seen the Ukrainian rite performed. After the service, Bishop Legal spoke to the congregation in English. There were a large number of Ukrainians assembled—Greek Catholics, Roman Catholics and Orthodox—who had arrived in Alberta that year. All of them were overjoyed that at long last they could welcome their own priest to the settlement.

Bishop Legal appealed to the people to unite in supporting the Catholic faith and in organizing a parish. He offered to try to get free land from the government for a church and cemetery. That day many signed up as members of the first Ukrainian Greek Catholic parish. During the winter they collected lumber and by the summer of 1898, there stood a church in the school district of Limestone Lake. To this day there remains a Ukrainian cemetery near the Star railway station. That church was built by D. Glukhy and Ivan Matii, both of whom were probably Roman Catholics from Galicia.

That summer, while the church was being built, a second Ukrainian Greek Catholic priest, the Reverend P. Tymkiewicz [Tymkevych], visited the settlement from the United States and quickly returned.

The First Ukrainian Carollers in Alberta

Ivan Romaniuk recalls that during Christmas the first group of carollers got together at Beaver Creek [to raise funds] for the completion of the church building. The group was organized by Ivan Pillipiw and the director of the singing was Ivan Romaniuk, Mykhailo's son, who later lived on a farm near Myrnam, Alberta. His father lived in Chipman. This was the first group of carollers in Canada to spread Ukrainian songs across the wide expanses of the Beaver Lake and Beaver Creek districts of northern Alberta. Most of the carollers were from the same village, Nebyliv, and they did not miss anyone as they went carolling from house to house collecting money for the church.

From the summer of 1898 until June 1900 not one Ukrainian priest appeared among the Ukrainian settlers in Canada, either from the United States or from the Old Country. The old-timers in Manitoba used to say that in 1899 a Reverend [Damaskian] Polyvka from Galicia passed through Winnipeg on his way to the United States, but he did not visit any of the settlements.

Without their priests, the Ukrainian settlers were forced to turn to foreign clergy such as Protestants and Roman Catholics for their religious needs, but the most sought-after were the Russian priests, who did not even charge a fee. This situation gave the Russian missionaries a golden opportunity to influence the settlements.

The communities split into different religious factions with, for example, Pavlyna being baptized by a Roman Catholic priest, while at the neighbour's Mykhailo would be baptized by a Protestant and at another neighbour's Vasylyna would be baptized by a Russian Orthodox priest. It also happened that whenever a clergyman appeared in the community he would marry Ukrainians and baptize their children, be they Greek Orthodox, Greek Catholic or Roman Catholic. But there were some who said, "We're not going to have our children baptized until our own priests arrive. Surely in that time they won't grow horns. And if they do, we'll knock them off. We'll not accept a foreign faith."

The Beginning of Religious Problems in the Settlements

By 1900 rumours had spread among the Ukrainian settlers in Canada that Ukrainian Greek Catholics would not get their own priests from Galicia because Rome would not allow married priests to go to Canada, and that the Orthodox would not get their own priests from Bukovyna because the Russian Orthodox priests were there already. Neglected, there was nothing for the settlers to do except to choose whatever denomination they wanted.

In Alberta, in 1899, for example, the settlers asked Anton Sawka [Savka], a deacon from Peremyshl, Galicia, who lived in Beaver Creek, to write to the Russian Bishop Nykolai [Nicholas] of San Francisco to send a permanent missionary to the Ukrainians in Alberta, because the communities were expanding, children were growing up unbaptized and young people were living together without marriage vows. It was said that the Orthodox bishop responded with a very favourable letter saying he would send them not one but two missionaries, but he did not say when or from where. Unfortunately, no copy of either letter is now available. They have been lost forever. The Ukrainians most concerned were the Greek Catholics from Galicia, who had lived in the Beaver Lake and Beaver Creek colonies since 1894.

Father Lacombe Goes to Rome

The Roman Catholic bishop in Alberta, Legal, quickly sized up the situation among the Greek Catholics and sent his faithful priest Father Lacombe to Rome to explain the problem. In fact, the Ukrainian settlers in Canada were on the verge of a major religious upheaval. Some were thinking about organizing a "Ukrainian Independent Church"; others were joining, as they put it,

"Orthodoxy"; a third group was becoming "Latinized"; others were leaning toward Protestantism or becoming "Socialists."

From Rome, Father Lacombe went to Vienna and from there to Lviv in Galicia, where he held discussions with the young Metropolitan Andrii Sheptytsky, who, at Father Lacombe's suggestion, sent a Greek Catholic priest, the Reverend I. Zaklynsky, to Canada for the Ukrainians in Alberta. The following year, 1901, the Reverend [Vasyl] Zholdak, the secretary of the consistory in Lviv, came to Canada to examine the state of affairs.

His visit aroused interest among Ukrainian Greek Catholics in America as well as Canada, where Reverend Zholdak visited almost all the larger Ukrainian communities and promised that as soon as he returned to the Old Country, he would take appropriate steps to have the consistory send more priests. But he did not say what kind of priests.

During Reverend Zholdak's visit to Canada, Reverend Zaklynsky was already settled in Alberta. At the same time the long-awaited Russian missionary, the Reverend Iakiv Korchinsky, arrived from Alaska. This marked the beginning of religious strife among the Ukrainian Greek Catholics in Canada.

The Court Battle Over the Church at Star, Alberta

The trouble among the settlers (most of whom were from the same village) over the church building at Beaver Creek began with a very simple but thoughtless action. For the Easter services in 1901 one part of the congregation of the first Ukrainian Greek Catholic church invited Reverend Zaklynsky, while another part invited Reverend Korchinsky. Although they had split into Catholics and Orthodox earlier, they had not interfered with each other's priests, provided the two priests did not minister to them on the same Sunday. They had not interfered because the church had been built by common effort. But when Easter came each group wanted priority.

The Greek Catholics insisted that when the church was being built everyone understood that it was Greek Catholic. The other side argued that it was Greek Orthodox because the first service conducted in it was by a Russian Orthodox priest, and so they had the first say. They fought over this issue so much that that holy time turned out not to be an Easter at all, because neither Reverend

Zaklynsky nor Reverend Korchinsky was allowed to enter the church.

The people lined up in rows on opposite sides of the church with the Easter bread they had brought to be blessed. They yelled at and ridiculed each other so much that one was ashamed and scandalized to listen to them. And from then on, they began to hate each other, which led right to the courts, first in Edmonton, then Ottawa and finally all the way to London, England.

The proceedings lasted almost four years and cost over $75,000. There were over sixty church members in all but only twenty-six bore the court costs, because some left the congregation before it was all over while others joined the Roman Catholic church.

The Basilian Fathers in Canada and the Transfer of Churches to a "French" Corporation

As soon as Reverend Zholdak returned to the Old Country, he advertised among the Greek Catholic priests for volunteers to go to Canada. It was rumoured in Canada that fifteen secular priests in Galicia had applied at the consistory in Lviv for information. Why none of them ever came to Canada is still a mystery. Instead, in 1902 three Basilian fathers named P. Filias, S. Dydyk, A. Strotsky and a brother, I. Ianishevsky, and four nuns arrived. In the fall of 1903 two more monks came, M. Hura and N. Kryzhanovsky. The former group went to Alberta to be under the jurisdiction of Bishop Legal, while the latter group remained in Winnipeg under Archbishop Langevin.

These young Ukrainian missionaries began their work so enthusiastically that, instead of improving the situation among the Greek Catholics they seemed to make it worse, all because churches were signed over to a "French" corporation called "The Corporation of Greek Ruthenian Catholics United to Rome." In order to get rid of their competition—the Russian priests who were by this time well-entrenched among Ukrainian Greek Catholics in the settlements—the Basilian fathers began to demand almost forcefully that communities sign over their church buildings and cemetery lands to the corporation. The Russian priests made no such demands, and the sudden drive for signatures upset even the most faithful, who suspected that the Basilian fathers had come to Canada to further Latinization among Ukrainian Greek Catholics.

They would say, "Why else would the French want our church property if not to get us into their clutches."

The Basilian fathers met the stiffest opposition wherever the Russian missionaries were already rooted, or where there were settlers who had defended the Ukrainian church against Polish Jesuits in the Old Country, or where there was a faction holding radical views. As well, the settlers did not know anything about "monks" in the Ukrainian church. These were known only in the Roman Catholic church, never in the Ukrainian Catholic one. The monastic order of St. Basil had existed among the Ukrainians in Galicia only in very recent times, from about 1882, and not everyone in the villages was aware of it. So when the Ukrainian monks appeared in Canada, they were considered traitors and were called "wolves in sheep's clothing."

"Bishop" Seraphim in Canada

At the time the Basilians came to Canada, there also appeared from somewhere a Russian "bishop" called Seraphim, whose last name was Ustvolsky. In Winnipeg he began to organize the Independent Ukrainian Orthodox church, which would be neither under the jurisdiction of Rome nor Moscow. The Ukrainians in the United States were thinking along similar lines and the idea of an independent church also interested Ukrainians in Canada. What added to this interest was everyone's expectation that secular married priests would come to Canada, the kind familiar to them in the Old Country. Instead they got celibates, and the question of celibate versus married clergy sparked a lively debate everywhere, with resulting chaos.

"Bishop" Seraphim had come at the right time and all the enthusiasts of independence quickly accepted him into their midst. He ordained the leaders as "priests," who, in turn, were welcomed with open arms by fellow believers in the settlements. The first organizer of the Independent Ukrainian church to be ordained was Theodore Stefanyk of Winnipeg, followed by Ivan Bodrug, Ivan Negrich, Mykhailo Bachynsky and many others in the colonies. The Seraphim movement spread very quickly and people would have been really interested if only Seraphim had been a real bishop.

It turned out later, however, that he was simply a defrocked Russian priest, an imposter. When his clergy realized that they had been misled, some got rid of their vestments and clerical collars, while others became Protestants. From the Seraphim movement, a Protestant church began among the Ukrainians that survived for a while, then collapsed. Although it tried from the very beginning to attract the disaffected followers of Seraphim, it failed because those who believed in the Ukrainian Independent church always dreamed of Ukrainian independence in matters of church and state: an independent church in Canada and an independent state in Europe.

~5~

The Birth of "Socialism" Among Ukrainians in Canada

Religious problems among the colonists had to a certain extent demoralized the people, both on the farms and in towns. Some individuals had been accused of radicalism earlier, but they were in fact religious people. Just as there were those in the Old Country who despised authoritarianism in the churches, there were also those in Canada who would not put up with impudent sermons—be they Catholic, Orthodox or Protestant—sermons without true piety and with only partisan arrogance. Often a priest of one Ukrainian church group would tactlessly attack his rival in another church, even though there were Ukrainians and relatives in both.

Fanatical obstinacy, intolerance and arrogance among the religious leaders did not foster a noble spirit in the Ukrainians forsaken in the new land. On the contrary, it generated its opposite, and so the more enlightened people began to criticize all the "missionaries" who raced in from all directions to save the Ukrainian soul in Canada while pouring abuse upon each other. Like today, those who dared to disagree with such "teachings" and would not attend church were labelled "socialists" by the clergy.

Every year the number of these "socialists" increased, because new immigrants continued to arrive in Canada and among them were an ever-growing number of enlightened young people. In order to prove that they were really interested in the fate of their less fortunate brothers in this foreign land, these "socialists" began to organize reading rooms [*chytalnyi*] in educational societies [*prosvity*]. And such a "socialist" society was first organized in Edmonton in 1903, probably in Paul [Pavlo] Rudyk's store on Kinistino Street.

In Winnipeg, in 1904, a group of young Ukrainian progressives got together in the home of the immigration agent, Cyril Genik, where they staged the drama *Svatannia na Honcharivtsi* [Courtship at Honcharivka]. In 1905 the leaders of this group held a meeting in Edinger's office to form an educational society. Although they had as yet no facilities, they met wherever they could, read together and discussed their own fate and that of their brothers on this side of the ocean.

Edinger, a German from Bukovyna, sold real estate in Winnipeg. He saw that these young Ukrainians needed a community hall [a *narodnyi dim*: literally, a national or people's home] where they could gather, and so he built a hall at his own expense at the corner of Selkirk and MacGregor Streets. This was the first Ukrainian community hall in Winnipeg. Later Father Hura bought it to establish the Greek Catholic community hall. He did this because there was a reading room at the Basilian church and, to clip the radicals' wings, he had to chase them out of the neighbourhood.

Not to be outdone, the "socialists" found a place at the Baptist church on Manitoba Avenue, just a few blocks north of Selkirk Street. Later they bought this church from a businessman, a Jew named Zaltsman. At that point, internationalism crept into their ranks. Paul Crath [Pavlo Krat] brought it to Canada from Russian Ukraine, but the "socialists" were not attracted to his ideology. In 1907 they broke with the internationalists and formed a group of Ukrainian nationalists under the leadership of T. D. Ferley [Ferlei]. To this day they are located in their own home, the Ukrainian community hall on Burrows Avenue.

In Edmonton the first "socialist" reading club ceased to exist because its leadership dispersed among the coal mines of Alberta and British Columbia. It was replaced by a non-socialist one organized at the Greek Catholic church on Namao Street. In 1918 this group built its own hall on 109th Avenue. Some members of the first group tried to form an educational society, but they lacked the resources until students and enlightened young people finally formed the Ivan Franko Drama Circle, which led to the establishment of the Mykhailo [Michael] Hrushevsky Ukrainian

Institute in Edmonton.

Problems in Organizing Schools in the Settlements

The Ukrainians who settled on the expanses of the great Canadian West were poor. The difficulties they encountered on the wide prairie can be imagined from the scant reminiscences included here. First they worried about safeguarding themselves and their families from starvation. Then they got involved in religious debates, but they never forgot another pressing and essential issue—education for their growing children.

Those who concerned themselves most with schooling were individuals who understood its importance in a foreign country. As if it was not enough that the majority of colonists were illiterate, the number of their children growing up in Canada increased steadily. The situation appeared the most difficult among Ukrainian colonists because they settled in forests where it was difficult to make a living, where roads were almost nonexistent and where social life was pathetic. It was thus quite a few years before some in scattered places began to think about schools for their children. Immigration flowed so quickly into Western Canada that the provincial departments of education could not find enough qualified English teachers.

Other nationalities who came to Canada in an organized manner had ministers and teachers, many with higher education. This was not the case with the Ukrainians, among whom were very few who could take on the role of priest or teacher. There were areas where it was hard to find anyone capable of organizing a Ukrainian school, let alone a public school. For this, one had to have a command of English, and in the beginning there were very few such Ukrainians. It is said that in Manitoba it was Cyril Genik who first learned English, followed by Theodore Stefanyk, who became an interpreter. We are not certain who was the first Ukrainian in Saskatchewan to translate from Ukrainian into English, but it was said that Petro Shvydky from St. Julien was most concerned with interpreting. In Alberta the English language was spoken by Messrs. Killyar, Paul Rudyk and Michael Gowda [Mykhailo Govda] in Edmonton; Peter Svarich in Vegreville, Andrew Shandro in Whitford and Theodore Nemirsky in Wostok. Eventually, interpreters in the cities increased so much that the settlers coming to town had a hard time dodging them. They all wanted to serve, but how was one to pay them.

Right from the start, in areas where there were already English, German or French settlers, there was no problem with schools, but wherever there were exclusively Slavic settlements that had never heard or understood a word of English, there were problems. An interpreter was absolutely essential to get information from the government on how to organize a school district in Canada.

This difficult situation was resolved most quickly by the government of Manitoba. It appointed school organizers, whom the pioneers called "inspectors." These organizers had to know at least two languages, English and their own or another. They travelled to places where there were no schools, organized school districts and built centrally located schools.

Among Ukrainians, the first school organizers were a Pole named John Baderski and a Ukrainian named Theodore Stefanyk. About 1910 they were joined by Paul Gigeychuk [Pavlo Gigeichuk]. In Saskatchewan Joseph [Osyp] Megas, Mykyta Romaniuk, Mykhailo Kun* and, likely, Julian Androchowicz [Iulko Andrukhovych] did similar work, all paid by the government. In Alberta there were no education officers of non-English ancestry. Mr. R. Fletcher, a farmer from Lamont, was the school organizer for foreigners in Alberta. If he needed an interpreter, he either brought one with him or looked for one in the district. He used the services of the following Ukrainians: Theodore Nemirsky in Wostok, Andrew Shandro in Whiford, Wasyl Hawrelak [Vasyl Havryliuk] in Wasel, Ivan Letavsky in Lamont and Peter Svarich in Vegreville.

The Ruthenian Training School in Winnipeg

Organizing school districts was difficult not only among Ukrainian settlers but also among other immigrants in Western Canada, and organizing a school district was only half the problem; it was even more difficult to maintain the school. Not only were the settlers poor and unable to hire a teacher year-round, but it was also hard to find qualified teachers. And even if there were

---

* The reference is likely to J. Kuhn of Yorkton who, like Androchowicz of Vonda, was a "supervisor of Schools in Foreign-Speaking Districts," 1914–17. (Ed.)

teachers, half of them taught on permit.*

At the time there were no roads in the settlements and children had to walk through bush, swamp and forest. In winter there was no school because it was too cold and in summer, even if the school opened, more than half the children stayed home. The older children helped with the hard pioneer work and the younger ones were afraid to go alone two or three miles to school through the bush. What added to their reluctance was their inability to understand the teacher. In most cases those who taught on a permit were either veterans of the Boer War or English students working during the summer to earn enough money to further their education in the winter.

They were not pedagogues but simply "lumberjacks," as our people called them. Those who were qualified teachers in the province naturally preferred to teach among their own people rather than in districts full of poverty-stricken foreigners, where the pay was low and life full of hardships. In the rural districts the pay of teachers ranged from thirty to forty-five dollars per month, out of which they had to pay room and board. Usually they stayed at a farmer's place, often living with the family in a single room. There were instances where three teachers taught in the same school during a single year. One taught one month and left; another came but did not last long either and so on. Teachers went from district to district looking for a "better" school, but they were all the same. They did not look for a nicer school building or nicer students but for more convenient living quarters. Sometimes the teacher lived two or three miles from the school, and when it came to treading through mud one no longer felt like teaching. With the summer heat, a teacher would let the children out for recess or lunch and fall asleep at the desk. Time flew and those who suffered most were the young who grew up without an education. The people in the settlements finally complained to the government that they were paying school taxes without getting any benefits.

To improve the situation, the provincial government, which was responsible for the situation in the first place, became concerned, but so also did the more intelligent Ukrainian people and other settlers in Canada, who saw how Ukrainian youth was being

---

* Individuals who lacked qualifications to teach were given special permits by departments of education. (Ed.)

wasted. Ukrainian immigrants were discriminated against everywhere. Exploited and slandered as the worst of all the immigrants, they were compared to the Indians because they were the poorest to come to Canada and did not know the language. With their children growing up without an education or knowledge of English, they too would someday face the same bitter situation. It was in Manitoba that they first convinced the government to open up a special teachers' course for Ukrainian boys who had secondary education in their own language.

The Ukrainian college, called the Ruthenian Training School, was on Minto Street in Winnipeg. At first twenty-two students registered and by the end of the year there were thirty-eight. The students called it the *bursa* [a resident boarding school]. Mr. Percy Cressey, an Englishman from Yorkshire, was the principal. The lower grades were taught by A. Chisholm, a Canadian, while Ukrainian was taught by Iakiv Makohin, a Ukrainian from Galicia who had graduated from high school in Chernivtsi in Bukovyna. They were all paid by the provincial government.

The following year, without any explanation at the time, the government replaced I. Makohin with an elementary school teacher from Lemkivshchyna in Galicia, D. D. Pyrch. He had come to Canada from Shamokin, Pennsylvania. In 1909 the school was transferred* to Brandon, Manitoba, because the good people of Winnipeg had informed the government that students at the school were getting too involved in politics. It should be remembered that Winnipeg was already a metropolis of central Europeans, who envied the Ukrainians' good fortune in getting the Ruthenian Training School from the Conservative government of Manitoba.

The school was meant to prepare young Ukrainians to be pioneer teachers who would teach English to "undesirable" central Europeans, a task the English teachers could not or would not do for children whom they called "Galicians."** Until there were Ukrainian teachers among the central Europeans on the farms, the teaching of English to children of early immigrants of Slavic origin was very slow. The schools that existed looked very neglected and the children displayed no interest in attending. They would teach "the dog, the cat, the boy," but there was no one to explain the words to the children. The English teacher did not understand the

---

* The school was transferred in 1907. (Ed.)
** To Czumer, the term "Galician" was strictly pejorative. (Ed.)

children, and they did not understand him. It is no wonder that one English missionary teacher once wrote in an English religious journal that the children of the central Europeans were so stupid that one could not expect them to become good and desirable citizens of Canada. The *Winnipeg Free Press* supported the opinion and even suggested halting the immigration of central Europeans to Canada.

At the time the bilingual system existed in the public schools of Manitoba, Saskatchewan and Alberta.* Alongside English, children could be taught in their native language. In the early years of Ukrainian immigration the system was the salvation of Ukrainian children because there were not enough qualified English teachers to fill the schools, and children were taught in their own language. The French and the German colonists took the most advantage of the opportunity because they had many teachers and ministers who could teach. If they did not know English, they substituted their own language. But it was difficult for Ukrainians to do the same because Canadian "patriots" thought central Europeans would "Balkanize" the country.

It was to improve the above situation that Messrs. Rudnytsky and Kosovy, two Ukrainian intellectuals who lived in Winnipeg, had advised the Government of Manitoba in 1904 to establish a special teachers' programme for young, intelligent Ukrainian boys who already had some secondary education in their own language but no opportunity to learn English because they lacked finances. The suggestion was wise and timely and, in spite of strenuous opposition, the government acted by opening a three-year programme in 1905. By the end of June 1907 the school graduated twenty-eight Ukrainian-English teachers in Manitoba. They were dedicated individuals to whom we must be grateful for the educational advances they spurred among young Ukrainians in Canada.

How the First Ukrainian-English Teacher Obtained a Position in Manitoba**

At the end of 1907, when our teachers' course finished, Mr. Baderski visited the *bursa*, the Ruthenian Training School in Winnipeg, and

---

* Although bilingual classes existed in Saskatchewan and Alberta, between 1897 and 1916 they were official only in Manitoba. (Ed.)
** Although not indicated in the original text, this is Mr. Czumer's own story. (Ed.)

proposed a job at school "B" for anyone who could speak four languages, i.e., English, Polish, Ukrainian and German. There were several others besides myself who knew those languages, but they declined the offer. It didn't appeal to their good sense for a young teacher to go into a quarrelsome district to try to please ratepayers of various nationalities, even though the district wasn't bad since it was near the town of Beausejour. Once I finally decided to accept Baderski's offer I never regretted it. It's probably the nicest district of Ukrainians from Galicia that I've ever come across in Western Canada.

John Baderski notified the trustees of school "B" that he had found the kind of teacher they wanted and that he'd come in the middle of August to see about the contract. On 19 August I took a train from Winnipeg and within an hour and a half I was in town seeing the school secretary. I introduced myself and he introduced me to his wife. I found out that everything was going well, except that I would encounter problems with the chairman because he couldn't agree to having a "Galician" teach in their school. He was backed by five other Germans. Here I was speaking with the school secretary, who was also a German, but he wasn't worrying about school affairs. Although he had been living in the area, he had decided to live in town as a retired farmer.

I thanked the secretary for his information and started to walk the three miles north of town to the nearest trustee, also a German, to get his views. I thought to myself, "What if he doesn't agree? Then all my effort will be in vain." But I kept on walking. It was Sunday afternoon and I found him at home with his family, which consisted of himself, his wife and eight children. They all took a lively interest in me, as if they were greeting the new *schullehrer*. This was especially true of the children because their former teacher was an old German Baptist preacher, who wasn't liked by any children in the district, the German included. This young "Galician" boy, healthy as a cucumber, knows German, too! At that point I realized that I'd certainly get the teaching job in the district, even if there were obstacles thrown up by the chairman. The Polish trustee [Baderski?] had announced everywhere that a new teacher was coming, a Ukrainian, who had just finished teachers' college and knew the language of the ratepayers in the district. Eighty per cent of them supported the "Galician," although they hadn't even seen him yet.

The next evening the trustees gathered at the school house, and the secretary arrived from town to draw up the contract. Although he came to the meeting, the chairman stood by his conviction, saying, "There are no accusations against the former teacher other than that he's an old man. As far as his teaching goes, no one can fault him." This was his personal view and that of a few other Germans. But the majority disagreed and wanted to change the teacher. This generated a long debate among the trustees. The secretary and I went outside to give them a better chance to talk, because the argument was heating up. Outside, you could hear the loud discussion inside the school, with the chairman declaring that he, too, was not against changing the old teacher for a new one, but he couldn't agree to a "Galician" teaching his children.

When I heard this, I immediately walked in and appealed to the chairman's sense of reason. My diplomacy so disarmed him that there was nothing left for him to do except to sign or leave, and he agreed to sign.

I began teaching on 1 September 1907. Almost all the children of school age attended—only the Prussians wouldn't send their children because they were boycotting the "Galician" teacher. They sent them to the neighbouring school "GB," where the teacher was a German.

I'm not going to say much about social life in that community, because it was the same everywhere. I'll just say that in the following year all the German children of school age came, and they attended even more regularly than the others.

The first "Galician" Christmas in district "B". In my second year in the district I decided to organize a Christmas evening in the school, the first of its kind in that area. I asked the trustees for funds and they allocated twenty-five dollars from the school budget to buy presents, candies and nuts for the children. With this money I bought presents in Winnipeg for all the children in the school. I numbered them appropriately and during the concert they sat on a decorated table in front of the blackboard. After the concert, the children drew numbered tickets and Santa presented each with the corresponding gift on the table.

The school room was beautifully decorated with an evergreen and coloured paper chains so that everything looked festive. The concert took place the day before Christmas Eve, starting precisely at 7:00 in the evening and lasting till 10:30 p.m. The programme consisted of Christmas carols and recitations in English, Ukrainian, Polish and German. The master of ceremonies was the chairman of the local school board, a German from Galicia. So many people from the area came to this first "Galician concert" that the school room was absolutely jammed. Out of curiosity, even a few people came from Beausejour, including two English officials: the mayor and the chairman of the school board. They wanted to see for themselves what the "Galician" teacher, whom the taxpayers of school "B" spoke of so highly, could do. They were seated as special guests in the front row.

The teacher introduced the programme by explaining the purpose of the evening, and then the programme began. The first carol "Silent Night" was sung in English by all the children. This was followed by

"Coz to proze za nowina" [What News Is This] sung by the Polish children. Then the Ukrainians sang the traditional carol "Boh Predvichny" [God Eternal], and finally the German children sang "O Tannenbaum" [O Christmas Tree]. Scenes from the Christmas story were acted out after each song. It was a contest of songs from four nations and the first and most unusual Christmas concert ever held in a rural school in Western Canada to that time. The obvious interest and enthusiasm of the children as they sang their native carol and the delight of the public proved how pleasing the whole thing was.

At the end of the programme, "Santa" first distributed the gifts to the school children and then the nuts and candies to all the children and adults present. There was no end to the happiness that evening. Everybody praised the children for their performance and were amazed by the teacher's inventiveness in producing such a novel programme. The teacher thanked the audience for turning out in such large numbers, the ladies for their work in decorating the school, the children for their good behaviour and performance in carolling and the trustees for the children's gifts.

The mayor of Beausejour asked to say a few words:

"Ladies and Gentlemen. I'm fifty-four years old and attended school in old England, I've seen many a school in Canada and have served as a school trustee for a long time, but I must confess that I've never seen such a wonderful and exceptionally interesting school as this one of yours. This evening your children and their teacher had so enchanted me that I forgot where I was. Tears came to my eyes and I had to force myself not to burst out crying like an old lady in church when the minister delivers a moving sermon.

"The whole time I was deeply moved. I marvelled at and admired the lovely arias which your children sang so beautifully. I watched the co-ordination and co-operation between the students and their teacher, and without flattering you, because you all know me very well, I must say I never realized that Galicians had such beautiful songs.

"I still feel unnerved, excited by the impression your children and teacher made on me. Right at the very beginning of the concert, when they sang "Silent Night," which I know so well, it made me remember the Old Country, when I as a little boy ran carolling with the other children from house to house, for which we each received a penny. Not only did I remember, but I was more amazed and admired how masterfully and melodiously your children sang that carol, as if they had been born in England. Words fail me in describing my amazement. I'm ashamed to admit that today is the first time in my life that I've ever heard Galician Christmas carols. Although I didn't understand the words, the aria spoke for itself. I never imagined you had such nice carols. But what fascinated me most was how one teacher could teach children to sing so well in four languages. For English people it is rare to know several languages. I see, ladies and gentlemen, that you have talented children and a good teacher.

"I had heard about your school and your new teacher and I was interested, so today I came down especially with a friend because there was talk in town that you would be having a "Galician" Christmas concert. On my way to the concert tonight I told my friend about your children and how two years ago I was passing by your school and they were on the road (most likely it was recess) making mud pies and throwing them at me as if they were just snowballs. I treated it as a joke, but I thought to myself that they lacked manners and discipline. Today I'm convinced that this was during the time of their old teacher, the preacher. Today all my doubts about poor discipline in your school have vanished. And I want to tell you that I'd like to see the same harmony, co-operation and organization in our school. In conclusion, I'd like to congratulate your teacher and your children for their exemplary behaviour and beautiful concert. In town I'll tell people what a wonderful school you have." Applause!

Immediately after the speech the audience sang *Mnohaia lita* [May You Be Blessed With Many Years] in unison, as if they had planned it. It was interesting that it wasn't only the Ukrainians who sang, but also the Poles and Germans from Galicia. The Prussians, who had boycotted the teacher from Galicia, now congratulated him and personally gave him Christmas presents. The Ukrainians, who had felt like third-class citizens in the district, stood up straight and raised their heads in pride. They were proud of their countryman. He didn't act like a "foreigner" or some ignoramus but showed himself to be in charge of the school and a leader in the vicinity, in spite of the fact that the majority of the population was not Ukrainian.

Honour to Whom Honour is Due

Indeed, these first Ukrainian-English teachers from the so-called "School for Foreigners" were not only fine teachers, but leaders in the Ukrainian settlements of Western Canada. They were young people with a secondary education who knew their duty. It was as if God had meant them to enlighten those poor, downtrodden Ukrainians whom the Old Country considered lost. They worked among the settlers with great dedication, not restricting themselves just to school children but working with adults as well. Their appearance gave birth to a new spirit. Social life improved. They became true leaders, teachers and defenders of their downtrodden brethren. Everywhere they endeavoured to raise the knowledge of the Ukrainian colonists. They wanted to see their brethren in Canada in first place or at least equal to the civilized peoples who lived in this great country. They laid the foundations for social coexistence among the Ukrainian colonists and also made sure that the Ukrainian settler became a worthy and outstanding citizen, so that the young Ukrainian would not be neglected or become a footstool for others. Their dedication found admirers not only among the more far-sighted Ukrainian farmers and workers but also among non-Ukrainians. They were viewed as great workers and patriots. In short, they awakened the Ukrainian pioneer from his lethargic sleep and neglect and pushed him into the whirlwind of Canadian life. They pushed him in the direction of learning and knowledge without which it would have been difficult for his descendants to live in Canada. Out of a frightened, downtrodden Galician-Ruthenian, these teachers created an aware Ukrainian Canadian. Just as the work of our pioneers on the farms was not wasted, so also the work of those first Ukrainian-English teachers of Ukrainian youth in Western Canada has been crowned with great success. The fruits of their labours are reaped a hundredfold today. Let us honour those to whom honour is due.

~6~

Ukrainian Labourers in Canada

We have mentioned the fortunes of rural settlers but said little about the Ukrainian urban workingmen. Because someday it may be of interest to know about the life of those who chose to stay in the city and there to raise their descendants, I would like to mention them, if only in outline form.

At the very beginning of immigration to Canada, Ukrainians came with the purpose of settling on the land. First they came to look around and get acquainted with conditions, and then they brought their families. Few Ukrainians came to Canada to work for wages. If anyone did have that in mind he went to the United States, where there was a demand for such labourers.

Not every Ukrainian immigrant had sufficient funds to support his family on the farm when he first arrived in Canada. He needed an additional job with a more prosperous farmer or on the railroad or in the city. Day-to-day necessity forced farmers to search for jobs wherever they could find them, so they could earn enough money to support their families on the farm.

Among the immigrants were men who came without families. When they got to Winnipeg, for example, they stayed to earn some money, find a homestead, bring their family out, or if they were bachelors, find a wife and settle down on a farm. But there were those who liked city life and stayed. The majority were bachelors who, having earned a few dollars either digging ditches or working on the railroad, remained in the city during the winter because they had no other home in Canada. These homeless single men formed the proletariat in Canada. As time passed, the number of urban workers in Western Canada increased with the arrival of new immigrants. The Ukrainians got the dirtiest and hardest jobs. They could not find other work because they did not understand the language. Undoubtedly, this is what made them unskilled labourers in Canada.

In 1905 Western Canada had a surplus of Ukrainian and other central European labourers. "Uncles"[vuiky], as the poor men from the countryside were called by our young people in the cities, also came into town looking for work. The name stuck for a long time. At times so many of these "workers" flooded into a city that there was not work for all and they wandered the streets in gangs attracting attention to themselves. From this came the expression "Poor Galicians." It was a sad situation because many of these "Poor Galicians" went hungry for weeks, without work and with their savings run out.

Often the wretched vagrants would be sent somewhere into the forest or far away by rail. If, for example, ten were needed, fifty were signed up and sent. The surplus then returned hungry and on foot to Winnipeg, Edmonton or Regina to wait for a job to turn up. They could not speak English and they could complain to no one. As the saying goes, "God is high above and the government is far away." And so the immigrant, without any protection, without knowledge of the country, a stranger in a strange land, with his family overseas or far away in the bush, felt totally deserted and suffered his dark fate silently.

Young people fared better. Nothing worried them and they could find work quicker than older men. One can imagine a group of workingmen arriving at a steam shovel on the railroad, the boss waving his hands and showing ten fingers, which meant he wanted only ten men and the young ones running and grabbing the shovels, leaving none for the older ones. Often they would lie by the dozens under the open sky on the prairie waiting days and shivering nights for that back-breaking work, but there was none. After a few days some returned hungry to their homes while others searched for work on the farms of those of other backgrounds. This is a poem about their situation:

In a Foreign Land

Seeking my fortune, ignorant of my fate, I wandered
Over wide expanses and high mountains, lost.
My heart and soul pierced by painful anguish and
oppressed by powerlessness.
You will perish in a foreign land without happiness or
hope, an ominous voice tells me.
Seeking my fortune, ignorant of my fate, I wandered
Over wide expanses and high mountains, lost.

D. Ia.

Some did not like Canada and these were more prevalent in the city than in the country. We will not dwell on the reasons for their dissatisfaction because there were hundreds. Those who could not stand it any longer either earned or borrowed money for a ticket home. Many went back or emigrated to the United States. One of those who was dissatisfied with Canada and returned home, wrote this poem:

You Are Not Mine, Canada

You are not mine, Canada dear!
Your riches are not for me;
There is no hope here,
You are not mine, Canada.

You are not mine, though your freedom is wide
Someone else will thank you;
But my years here will pass in vain,
You are not mine, Canada.

You are not mine, though you drew me like a magnet,
Someone else loves you, not me.
You will embrace him to yourself,
You are not mine, Canada!

You are not mine: for what have I got here?
What can I show off to you
Except all my hard suffering;
You are not mine, Canada!

You are not mine, generous country!
Even though your future shines,
My life here will always be bitter;
You are not mine, Canada!

"Puhach" 1905

The "No-Worry" Party

Ukrainian workers in western Canadian cities were divided into two groups. To one group belonged the intelligent and self-respecting people and to the second category those who could not care less about what happened tomorrow, as long as they had a good time. They were called the "no-worry" party or "jack-o-maniacs."

Because of the way things were in the city, a good, well-behaved boy very often would get involved with the vagrants. Perhaps a useless friend would drag him into the gang of drunken good-for-nothings and it would take some time for him to free himself. Nobody had any control over the young men or over the older either. They did not go to study classes or to church. In their free time they drank in the hotels and on Sundays they played cards at the railway station.

If these hooligans appeared in a hall or at a wedding, there was always an unpleasant disturbance. Often paddy wagons transported these "Galician boys" like sheep to jail, where they were held overnight for hearings. Often it was sheer stupidity rather than criminal behaviour that landed them in jail. For instance, one of these "Jacks" would have one too many and start to act smart. The proprietor would call the police to throw him out. The policeman would ask him politely to leave the hotel, but he would grab the policeman's shoulders to show how tough he was.

These "Jacks" were organized to rescue friends in trouble. Often this rescue would land all of them in jail, and on the front pages of the English morning-dailies one would read: "Bunch of Galician Boys Arrested," or "Police Wagons Busy Last Night," or "Big Fight at Galician Wedding."

This class of characters among Ukrainian workingmen brought disgrace upon all Ukrainians in Western Canada. It was difficult to get through to them—to socialize them—because the majority had no parental supervision in Canada, and when they earned some money they acted freely in the full sense of that word. These rogues constituted the first of the so-called "Galician boys."

To remedy the situation among these trouble-makers, enlightened individuals tried to establish an organization to educate the workingmen in the cities. It offered lectures on various topics, and the meetings did have some influence on those who came. The trouble was that not all the vagrants were anxious to join the educational society. It looked like a waste of time to them, so they clung to their "workingman" culture—drinking, partying and playing cards.

This is a satire on the "Jacks" that Stefan Fodchuk wrote in the newspaper *Novyny* [The News] in Edmonton in 1914:

Letter to the Immortal Fellowship of "Jacks" in Manipeg [Winnipeg]

Most Respected Fellows:

I sit at my desk, take up my pen and write to my friends. Wing your way little letter over hill and dale and when you get to Manipeg say "hi" to my immortal friends.

Beloved lads! I got your letter and am writing back immediately. Don't be mad for not hearing from me for so long as if something had shut me up. You see it's because of my stupid habit.

It was like this. God gave us a holiday and I said, well, if we have to celebrate, then let's do it right. And Mike immediately took the hint and came out with a dollar for a start. After Mike, God bless them, came Jim, Tony, Charlie, Bill and the others with their donations to the kitty. Even Petro the "Manigrant" gave a quarter, about which he will feel sorry for a year. No wonder, once a manigrant [immigrant], always a manigrant. What does he know! He doesn't even know how to eat on the gang. He'd come off the job and immediately spend the whole night going through books and newspapers like a deacon in the village. Will that reading do any good? At least since I bawled him out he doesn't read aloud anymore.

True, there are some good books. The other day the missus was reading about the prophetess Michalda. Boy, oh boy, it made me shiver with fear to hear about her. All kinds of weird things are going on in God's world and the Christian lives like a fly. But I'm rambling and I forgot to finish what happened to the holiday collection.

Anyway, enough was collected for two kegs of beer and a mickey of whisky, the kind that when you drink it your eyeballs pop out and for half an hour you can't say a word. We discussed who should go get it. The manigrant spoke up and said, who else if not Uncle Stefan. The others said nobody was ashamed because nobody knew them here.

I didn't want to make trouble on Ascension Day, but I could have socked him one. Maybe your dad's name was Stefan, but my name is Shtif [Steve], you manigrant in wooden boots! I threw my sack over my shoulder and trudged off to the liquor store for beer.

The clerk rolled out two kegs of beer for me. I put both of them in the sack so I wouldn't have to make two trips. I stuck the mickey in my hip pocket. The clerk hoisted the sack on my shoulders till my back creaked, and off I went. They roared with laughter and I thought to myself, "Laugh you idiots, you'd laugh at holy pictures just for a laugh."

So I hauled the beer, my eyeballs popping out of their sockets, sweat pouring down my forehead, my face as red as if, my brothers, I had just come out of the steam bath. I met Harry on the way and he says to me, "Hey Uncle, what are you carrying, Paska? [Easter bread]" I barely got to the house and flipped it under the bench. The floor shook. "To hell with the beer and everything," I cried out. "My guts have been turned upside down." I sat down barely able to breathe.

I don't know if I hurt myself lifting it or what, but the holiday was ruined. After the holiday I spent six weeks in bed and I've now asked John to bribe the foreman to get me a job because I'm stone broke. If I get a job I'll write you again about everything. Now I bow to you fellows a million times and adieu.

Sincerely yours,
"Shtif Tabachniuk"

This letter brings to mind those Ukrainian boys in Canada who had no shame and for whom it was necessary to resort to such columns to try to bring them to their senses. There were still other types among Ukrainian workingmen as illustrated in this story:

The Guest From Canada

Just before midnight, a train came to a stop in the magnificent Dniester River valley, lit by a full moon. Out of the coaches stepped several prosperous Jews and a man with a little box in his hands.

He went directly from the station to the road, then turned off on a path through the pastures, which led down a steep hill to the village of D... He obviously did not want to stop even for a second look at the mountains or to see how nice the village looked in the valley, how the cottages gleamed amid the orchards, how the Dniester sparkled wide and deep in the moonlight, and how a faint silver mist hung in the willows and the tall green birches. He was in a hurry or else he was insensitive to nature's beauty.

Not until he was in the village and on a small side street did he stop and begin to look around. About fifty paces in front of him stood a house with farm buildings, kitty corner was another house, and further beneath the hill among the trees it was dark and gloomy where the light from the moon did not shine.

Inside and outside everything was quiet. He stood there for a moment and then crept stealthily under the windows of the nearest house and peaked in a little window. He could not see or hear anything. He then put the box on the ground, grabbed the window frame and tried to force the window open. It did not budge.

Angry, he smashed the pane with his elbow. The glass shattered and someone cried out from inside the house, "Oh, my God!"

"Open up!" ordered the traveller in a stern voice.

"Who's there?" asked a frightened voice from inside.

"It's me, Iakiv, your husband!"

"Oh Lord! Iakiv! Right away! As soon as I get some light."

A small lamp flashed in the house and after a few moments the door opened. Iakiv went into the house with his box.

He neither greeted his wife nor said a kind word. He only looked around the house for a moment, sat down on a bench and looked angrily at his wife, who did not know whether to be happy or sad, she was so taken aback.

"Why did you break the window pane?" she asked meekly. He did not give her an answer. Instead he asked, "Is the child not here?"

"The child died the year you went to Canada. I wrote you about it."

"And where is the other one?"

"What other one? We didn't have another one."

"We didn't but you did!" Iakiv thundered. "I know all about it. I slave for three years across the ocean, day and night, while you gallivant around with somebody else. Tell me where the child is!"

The young woman, overworked, weary, but her face still beautiful, fixed her kerchief on her head and flashed an angry look with her dark eyes.

"There's no other child and never was!" she answered firmly. "And if you don't believe me, search!"

Iakiv rose to his feet. "You're going to talk back! They wrote me! What about that affair with Verbovy, the neighbour?"

"Lies! Lies!" she cried and turned to the door as if she wanted to run away. "I swear to God, it's a lie!"

At that moment her husband leaped at his wife and with all his might struck her with his fist on the back, grabbed her by the sleeve, tore her kerchief from her head and began beating her all over. She screamed and tried to tear herself from his grasp, but he held her with one hand tightly as with tongs and with the other beat her mercilessly.

"Help! Help!" she cried as she fell to the floor.

The doors to the porch and house flew open. On the threshold stood a robust peasant, Verbovy, with a fence post in his hands.

"What's this uproar in the middle of the night?" he yelled. "Is it you Iakiv? Is this the way you greet your wife and keep everyone awake?"

He put the fence post down and with one swing tore the crazed Iakiv from his wife, flinging him to the opposite corner with such force that Iakiv's head knocked a heavy bench farther into the corner.

"What a way to act!" he shouted again and with his legs spread far apart ready for a fight, he stood over Iakiv prepared at any moment to give him a bigger dose of his own medicine. But Iakiv leaped from the floor and took a swing at Verbovy, who grabbed both his hands, twisted them until they cracked and plunked the attacker down on the bench by the window.

"Sit and don't move! What do you want? What kind of trouble are you looking for?"

"You and my wife ... and you still beat me!" snarled Iakiv as he tried to free himself from his neighbour's powerful grip. The neighbour answered with a slap to his face that sent Iakiv sprawling.

"Don't lie, you son-of-a-bitch!" warned Verbovy.

"Three years you sat in Canada, without writing a word to your wife, without sending her a measly cent while she suffered here, barely able to stay alive, and yet as soon as you get back you start beating her. This is your present from Canada?"

"So she won't fool around with others!" Iakiv defended himself, but you could tell from the tone of his voice that he felt defeated.

"With whom?"

"You first of all! They wrote to Canada and told me."

Another resounding slap on Iakiv's cheek, which turned red and puffy.

"Who wrote?" asked Verbovy.

"Pidluzhny wrote."

"Don't lie. Pidluzhny can't write."

"He signed a letter someone else wrote for him."

"Fine. We'll ask him right now. Come on."

During this fiery exchange the battered woman moaned by the stove as if she was lamenting over a dead body.

"This is the reward I get for my hard work, for not selling one bit of land, for the numbness in my hands and legs. If in three years he'd sent some money—written a kind word—but nothing. Other husbands send money, bring back large sums, but he brings his fists."

"Don't cry, neighbour," said Verbovy, trying to cheer her up and pushing her husband onto the porch. "We'll be right back."

He dragged Iakiv outside and out on the dark street below the hill. The young woman followed them onto the road, where Verbovy's wife stood awakened by the shouting and fighting.

"My dearest neighbour, have you ever heard of such a thing? He came from overseas to beat me up for no reason, for nothing at all. In three years he didn't send me a measly cent, yet he's spent hundreds to get here to beat me up."

The neighbour calmed her down till she only sobbed like a little child as she leaned on the gate. Quite a few minutes went by on that dark street at the foot of the hill, until a solid slap echoed like the crack of a whip.

"So you came all the way from Canada to look for trouble," shouted

Pidluzhny so loudly that every word could be heard far away.

"Who wrote it then?" Iakiv said in a quiet, little voice defensively.

"What do I care? You have the letter, go find the writer. But don't bother people, you wandering gypsy. He's changed his clothes and thinks he's a somebody."

"Go to sleep," Verbovy told him, "and let people sleep and don't lay a finger on your wife or I'll be back."

Both neighbours walked Iakiv back to his house.

"Well, are you going to sleep or do we have to watch you?" asked Verbovy one more time.

"There's no need," answered Iakiv. He went into the house, picked up his box and came out again.

The neighbours watched what he would do. Without a word to anyone, the visitor from Canada walked down the street to the road and disappeared around a bend.

"I'll go after him," said his wife.

"Do you want to get killed?" asked Verbovy. She agreed. They all stood on the road for a long time and discussed this nocturnal adventure.

Meanwhile, Iakiv returned over the hill and pastures to the railroad station with his box in one hand and his other hand feeling his cheek. It was swollen and hot, and his head roared like a flourmill. Under his hat he found a big lump on his head from hitting the bench, and with his tongue he felt a loose tooth.

Dejected, he got to the station, put his box on a bench and sat down. He thought and thought, then took a bottle of whisky out of the box, took a big gulp and lost himself in thought.

He was discovered like this by a railroad worker, who was from the same village as Iakiv. He looked at Iakiv a couple of times but did not recognize him right away.

"Are you Iakiv?" he finally asked, "From Canada?"

"Yes," said Iakiv in English.

"Going home?"

"No." Those were the only English words he brought from Canada, and so he reverted to his own language. "I came home from Canada for a few hours to teach my wife a lesson and remind her that she has a husband. Did she have a baby or not?"

"No. I would have heard something."

"But I gave her such a thrashing that she won't forget. Three years, mind you. To have a wife and allow her free rein? Three weeks I travelled. I came, beat her and am going back to Canada. Three hundred crowns it cost and an equal amount to get back, but now she knows.

"What did you beat your wife for?"

"So she doesn't run around with other men," Iakiv answered.

"Looks like your face is swollen, probably you put on weight in Canada."

"Beat it!" yelled Iakiv angrily. "Don't bother me!"

Iakiv waited for an hour. Then he bought a ticket, got on the train that had come in, stretched out on a seat and began to snore as if he had just come out of a steam bath. Having done his duty, he returned to Canada. As for who had written the letter—that did not bother him anymore.

O.M.

When Things Got Better

It took quite a few years before the Ukrainian worker in Canada realized that making money and having a good time was not bliss for an immigrant in a foreign land. This kind of life could only appeal to the young and not for long. Intelligent and serious-minded people, especially those who had children, looked at life differently. They understood that without education their children would have to pay a heavy price in a foreign land. Because of circumstances, they began to organize themselves into associations of various kinds. Some were religious and considered that through the church the young would grow up obedient and retain native customs. Others had as their goal the education of those who had no parental supervision and organized educational societies. They attracted young single people by organizing entertainment for them or getting them to perform plays about the life of the people. In this way young Ukrainian boys and girls, especially those in the cities, spent their free time. They learned dramatic roles and Ukrainian songs which they sang in choirs. The most active in this area were young students who had had schooling in the Old Country.

There was a third group among the Ukrainian urban workers, whose goal was to raise the class consciousness and to struggle to improve the lot of the working class. They organized public meetings and appealed to workers to organize themselves into labour unions and make collective demands on their employers for better pay and working conditions. Such were the motives that gave rise to the organization of Ukrainian immigrants in Canada.

North Atlantic Trading Company advertisement beckons Ukrainians to Canada.

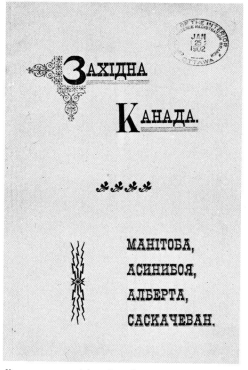

Canadian government immigration pamphlet in Ukrainian.

Ivan Pillipiw

Wasyl Eleniak

Joseph Oleskiw

Cyril Genik

Ivan Bodrug

Paul Crath

Sozon Dydyk

Nykyta Budka

Andrew Shandro

Paul Rudyk

Theodore Nemirsky

Peter Svarich

Roman Kremar

William Czumer (as a young man)

Taras D. Ferley and Iurii Syrotiuk

Burdei–Ukrainian pioneer's first home.

Ukrainian pioneer's second home, Northern Alberta, 1910.

Ivan Pillipiw's second home.

Home of Stefan Shandro, 1912.

Wedding reception at home of Andrew Shandro, Stefan's son, 1926.

Ukrainian pioneer women cutting logs prior to house building.

Hauling with oxen, Northern Valley, Alberta.

Bunk cars to house railway construction workers.

Interior of workers' bunkhouse.

(above) William Czumer's general store, Smoky Lake, Alberta; (left) Ukrainian National Co-operative Company, Vegreville, Alberta; (below) Ukrainian Narodnyi Dim (National Hall), Smoky Lake, Alberta.

First Russian Orthodox missionaries baptize children on Theodore Nemirsky's homestead, Wostok, Alberta, July 1897. *(Provincial Archives of Alberta)*

(left) First Ukrainian church in Alberta, built in 1897–8, subject of the famous Star court case; (centre) First Orthodox church, Pakan, Alberta, built in 1902; (right) Orthodox church at Wahstao, Alberta, built in 1915.

Ukrainian pioneer women, Wahstao church, 1941.

First Ukrainian Greek Catholic church, Winnipeg, 1904, ancestor of St. Vladimir and Olga Cathedral.

First class of the Ruthenian Training School in Manitoba c. 1905. *Front row* (left to right): M. Ostapovych, V. Maievsky, J. Hraban, W. Kohut, M. Basarabovych; *Second row*: T. Petryshyn, W. Czumer, V. Hrushov, V. Dedeliuk. J. T. Cressy (principal), M. Drabyniasty, D. Chisholm (instructor), W. Kolodzinsky, A. Klymkiw; *Third row*: J. Arsenych, I. Kotsan, C. Lytwyn, D. Yakimischak, J. Kulachkovsky, W. Karpets, G. Roshko; *Fourth row*: P. Ogryzlo, O. Hykawy, P. Chaikovsky, F. Hawryliuk, V. Saranchuk, P. Semotiuk.

Typical class of Ukrainian-English students at the Training School for Teachers for Foreign Speaking Communities, Regina (1909—17).

First convention of teachers and students of Ukrainian descent, Edmonton, 1915. Michael Luchkowich is in the second row, middle.

Committee for the Defence of the Ukrainian Language, Edmonton. 1913–14. In the first row, left, are Roman Kremar and William Czumer.

Ukrainian parents and children at first concert, South Kotzman School, Alberta, 1922.

First reading club (*chytalnia*), "Prosvita" Society, Myrnam, Alberta, established in 1909.

Members and children, Markiian Shashkevych Reading Club, Edmonton, 1914.

First Ukrainian Drama Club, Vegreville. Standing with book in hand is Peter Svarich.

Founders and first students, Taras Shevchenko Ukrainian Boys' Home (Bursa), Vegreville, Alberta, 1917.

Ukrainian immigrants arriving at Quebec City.

When and Where Ukrainian Organizations Began in Canada

Wherever Ukrainians settled, they tried to organize some kind of community group. Although without their own clergy, they were strongly religious and felt neglected without a church. They therefore got together in the most respected homes and often prayed or spent their leisure time discussing what to do about the future. These meetings in common became the basis of the various Ukrainian organizations in Canada, which began with the first Ukrainian settlements. Wherever there was a sizeable number of Ukrainians and conditions demanded a certain kind of organization, the pioneers got together to form religious, educational, political and economic groups.

The first church group was the Greek Catholic congregation formed in Beaver Creek, Alberta, in 1897. If our information is correct, its founder was Ivan Pillipiw, the first Ukrainian in Canada. Next came church congregations in Gonor and Stuartburn, Manitoba. In 1899 and 1900 their numbers increased substantially. They formed because of the need to acquire and register land for cemeteries in districts with large numbers of Ukrainians. Other organizations such as reading clubs [*chytalnyi*], drama clubs, educational societies [*prosvity*], fraternal clubs, labour organizations and community halls [*narodnyi domy*] began to appear one after another.

In 1903 the first reading club was formed in Edmonton. There are various opinions about who initiated it, but we do know that in 1904 it was the centre where the more enlightened people held their meetings. These were Paul Rudyk, Toma Tomashevsky, Iakiv Makohin, Ivan Letavsky and even Peter Svarich, back from Alaska, where he, along with English prospectors, had searched for gold. In 1907 members of the club performed a Ukrainian play under the direction of Michael Gowda. But the first amateur drama club among Ukrainians was organized by Peter Svarich in Beaver Creek, where a play was performed.

In 1904 an amateur drama group was organized to perform *Svatannia na Honcharivtsi* [Courtship at Honcharivka]. The founder and leader of the group was Ivan Antoniuk, a former high school student from Kolomyia in Galicia, who lived with Cyril Genik, the immigration agent in Winnipeg. Rehearsals were held in Genik's house on Euclid Avenue. Members of this group encouraged the formation of educational drama societies among the Ukrainians in Winnipeg and around the province.

The first "socialist" association among Ukrainians that even attracted older people was begun in 1905 by Antoniuk and other students from the Ruthenian Training School. The first concert in honour of the Ukrainian poet Taras Shevchenko was held in Winnipeg in 1906. Organized by students of the School, it was held in March at the Manitoba Hall on Logan Avenue. Ivan Antoniuk sang Shevchenko's poem "Hetmany" in a very smooth baritone, and D. D. Pyrch delivered an ill-prepared talk on the life of Shevchenko that left everyone dissatisfied.

Another early reading club was organized at the Basilian church by Father Hura. Under its auspices, Volodymyr Karpets and Nykola Hladky organized the Brotherhood of St. Nicholas, which was the first Ukrainian mutual benefit society in Canada. The first reading club among Ukrainian farmers in Manitoba was established in 1908 in Ladywood, originally called Brokenhead. It was organized by the Koziar brothers and V. Khraplyvy. The first lecture was delivered by W. A. Czumer, the teacher from Bachman School.

In Saskatchewan the first reading club, it was said, was established by the Vivchar brothers in Canora. From there later spread the movement for an "Independent Ukrainian Church," known as the "Church of Seraphim." In Alberta the first educational society was organized in 1910 by Pavlo and Petro

Melnyk and Vasyl and Ivan Romaniuk in Myrnam, sixty miles northeast of Vegreville. But the earliest organizations were church groups. By 1898 churches had been built in Gonor and Stuartburn, Manitoba, and Star, Alberta.

The first Ukrainian trading company was Zerebko [Zherebko] and Turcheniuk formed in Sifton, Manitoba, in 1905. Five years later the Brokenhead Farmers' Trading Company was organized by W. A. Czumer in Ladywood, Manitoba. That same year the Ukrainian National Co-operative Company was established by P. Svarich and Paul Rudyk in Vegreville, Alberta. A similar co-operative was then organized in Rosthern, Saskatchewan, by P. Shvydky. In Lamont, Alberta, there was another large company called Russian Mercantile, whose shareholders were all Ukrainians except for one German by the name of Schreyer, a native of Bukovyna. None of them survived commercially; some were sold to their managers while others went bankrupt. The company in Vegreville lasted the longest. It had branches in Radway, Chipman, Innisfree, Lamont, Andrew and Smoky Lake. It also had its own wholesale branch in Edmonton, which may have been the cause of its demise. The manager of the Brokenhead Farmers' Trading Company was V. Karpets and he survived the longest, over thirty-two years.

In 1909 the Ukrainian-English teachers organized the Ukrainian Publishing Company in Winnipeg to publish a Ukrainian newspaper for Ukrainians in Canada. The *Ukrainskyi holos* appeared in 1910 with T. D. Ferley as its first editor. When he was called to teach at the Ukrainian-English training school in Brandon, his place was taken by Wasyl Kudryk, while P. Woycenko [Voitsenko] became the publisher.

The creation of Ukrainian community halls in Canada began in 1907 when Father Hura bought Edinger's Hall at Selkirk and MacGregor for the Greek Catholics. Later Ukrainian socialists bought the old Baptist church on Manitoba Avenue and turned it into a "Labour Hall." Afterward, wherever there were reading clubs or theatre groups, community halls would eventually appear.

When these community halls had broken the ice, Ukrainians in places like Winnipeg, Saskatoon, Edmonton and even Vegreville decided to establish resident boarding schools or hostels [*bursy*] for students coming into the city to further their education. There they could get accommodation without having to beg their way into crowded non-Ukrainian hostels.

The first hostel was built in Edmonton in 1913 by Paul Rudyk. The first students to board there were N. Honsky, H. Novak and Ivan Melnyk. The place served as a community hall as well. On the first floor was a public hall for meetings and get-togethers, while the second floor provided living quarters for the students. When the Markiian Shaskevych Society built the Greek Catholic community hall in 1918 on 109th Avenue and the Mykhailo Hrushevsky Institute was established, also in Edmonton, Rudyk's residential school lost its original importance because it was a private venture. Rudyk sold it to the Ukrainian Workers' Association for the Ukrainian Labour-Farmer Temple.

Appeals to the People

To encourage Ukrainians to become members of reading clubs, drama circles, community halls and other organizations, leaders tried various slogans to arouse those people who did not care whether anything was happening.

At every opportunity, teachers in the rural areas reminded the settlers to send their children to school regularly. Their slogan was "In education lies our future." Always at meetings in the cities, the leaders of the progressive element appealed from the platform under another banner: "In organization and solidarity lies the power of the people." At the rural reading clubs of progressive farmers the call was "Knowledge will liberate the farmer and worker from bondage." Some harangued the proletariat with "Workers of the world unite!" Even the clergy had their slogan: "Faith in one church will save us in a foreign land." There is no doubt that every leader had good intentions and that such appeals did have some influence on those who found them interesting and meaningful. Unfortunately, there were those who either did not listen to anyone or who, for personal profit or interest, tried to sway the uncommitted to their side.

Others appealed to the people through the poems of Ivan Franko and Taras Shevchenko. The following poem by Franko was often used by the patriotic pioneers in Canada:

Awake, nation, arise.
Rise from your deep sleep!
Rise, open your eyes,
Rise at least in this time!

Awake, throw off your chains,
They are no longer for you to wear!
Show that you are able
To live without shackles and chains.

Only a slave bows
His back and his face!
What are you waiting for?
You have been a slave too long!

Nation awake, arise
You have been asleep too long.
Time to act,
To choose a brighter path.

The various groups fought heated battles on the pages of their newspapers. The first Ukrainian-language newspaper was the *Kanadiiskyi farmer*, published in Winnipeg in 1903. It was started by Liberal party politicians anxious to get the Ukrainian vote during elections. To counteract the Liberals, the Conservatives began to publish the Ukrainian newspaper, *Slovo* [The Word]. Each peddled its own line.

During the independent church movement in Western Canada, religious newspapers appeared: *Ranok* [Morning] published by the Presbyterians and another by the Russian Orthodox. There was also Seraphim's *Pravoslavny lystok* [The Orthodox Letter] (or some such title), and even a socialist newspaper for Ukrainian workers, *Chervonyi prapor* [The Red Flag].

By 1905 Ukrainians were divided into the following groups: Ukrainian Greek Catholics, Ukrainian Orthodox, Russian Orthodox, Independent Ukrainian Greek Catholics, followers of Seraphim, Presbyterians, socialists and populists. The first group was under the control of the Basilian fathers; the second was composed exclusively of Bukovynians; the third was those from Galicia who had Russian monks as their clergy; the fourth was those who refused to accept Basilians into their churches and demanded secular married priests. The Orthodox Ukrainians from Bukovyna sympathized with them. The fifth group consisted of Ukrainian "progressives" who considered both the Catholic and Orthodox churches backward and leaned toward Protestantism. The sixth group led by Paul Crath was made up of radical socialists for whom neither religion nor nationality counted for anything. Finally, there was a small group called *narodovtsi* [populists] or very often *Drahomanivtsi** or even radicals. They were not enthused with either socialism or any church group. They believed fervently that the only hope for the Ukrainian immigrant was education and national awareness and this they taught to people in other groups, which only roused the hostility of their leaders. The Basilians and bolsheviks hated them the most.

The populists were the greatest promoters of national consciousness among the Ukrainians in Western Canada. They defended the immigrant from unscrupulous individuals and pointed him toward a better future. Their leader was T. D. Ferley of Winnipeg.

Enlightened Ukrainians in each of the three Prairie provinces understood the significance of organization and acted accordingly. The associations they founded worked through reading clubs, lectures, plays, concerts and all kinds of entertainment, and their efforts attracted the attention of foreigners as well. Today the non-Ukrainian public considers these Ukrainian associations to be the Ukrainian people's representatives.

In Canada there are numerous Ukrainian associations. To date, the most important have been the community halls. In them, all have united, the young and old and people of different political and religious views—all who realized that they were part of one nation and that strength lay in organization.

These associations have carried on their work not only among their members, but also among educated nonmembers and informed others of the value of Ukrainian customs. The once scorned "Galician" grew in stature every year in the eyes of foreigners. Whenever there was an event, leaders would invite a prominent

---

* Mykhailo Drahomanov (1841–95) was a prominent Ukrainian scholar, political writer and editor who exercised a profound influence on the thinking and political orientation of the populists in Galicia. (Ed.)

Canadian from the province, who would then often write something positive about Ukrainians in the English press.

Not only community hall associations but Ukrainian teachers also conducted the cultural work, encouraging young people and school children to learn more. They often reminded them of the words of the great Ukrainain poet Taras Shevchenko who wrote:

Learn my brothers,
Learn and think;
Learn from the foreigner
But do not scorn your own.

For whoever forgets his mother
Will be punished by God;
Foreigners will scorn him
And not admit him to their home.

Ukrainians organized their educational societies and labour organizations much earlier in the cities than in the countryside, because the city offered more opportunities. Nevertheless, there were individuals in the rural areas concerned with the welfare of the people who did their best to introduce associations modelled on those in the cities. It was thus fascinating to see a Ukrainian play in the rural areas organized by an amateur who had seen a play in the city and tried to do something similar for his country neighbours. He got together everyone he could to form an amateur group that would stage a play or concert in honour of Taras Shevchenko, Ivan Franko or Markiian Shashkevych. Often the members of the group would be illiterate and the director would have to teach them their roles by heart. One really had to have a great deal of patience, devotion and determination to direct a play or even a concert, and you will not find that kind of determination among today's young people.

The Programme of the First Concert in Edmonton

You shall reign, Father
As long as there are people,
As long as the sun shines from the skies,
*They will not forget you.**

On Saturday, 14 March 1914, a commemorative concert sponsored by the Ivan Franko Dramatic Circle will be held in honour of the hundredth anniversary of the birth of the genius and prophet of the Ukrainian nation, TARAS HRYHOROVYCH SHEVCHENKO.

I

"Farewell to the Homeland," a piano solo by Mr. E. Anderson.
"Opening Remarks," Mr. B. Dedeliuk.
"My Thoughts," sung by a mixed choir.
"Saturdays," recited by Miss S. Seniuk accompanied by a mixed choir.
"My Spring Flowers," quartet.
"Don't Sing that Song to Me," solo by the well-known lyric tenor Mr. V. Steshyn with guitar accompaniment.
"What Good Are My Dark Eyebrows?" sung by the Shatulsky brothers.
"The Poplar," recited by Mrs. Tomashevsky.
"The Street," a medley of Ukrainian folk songs by the mixed choir.

II

"Who Was Shevchenko," an address by Mr. J. Yaremko [Iaremko].
"When Two Are Parting," a duet by V. Steshyn and J. Yaremko with piano accompaniment.
"On Easter Day in the Straw," a recitation by Miss Ie. Ferbey [Ferbei]
"The Sun is Setting," sung by the male choir.
"The Epistle," a recitation by Mr. D.Rostotsky.
"The Testament," sung by two mixed choirs with a bass solo.

The Concert will take place at the Conservative Club (formerly the old church) at the corner of Jasper and 103rd Street.
Piano Accompanist: Mrs. E. Anderson.
Choir Conductor: Mr. B. Dedeliuk.

---

* Excerpt from Shevchenko's poem dedicated to Ivan Kotlyarevsky, the father of modern Ukrainian literature. (Ed.)

Ukrainian Commerce Handicapped

Among Ukrainian settlers, the most handicapped undertaking was business, which the Ukrainian immigrant was not bold enough to attempt. On the farms Ukrainians were well-established economically; in the cities the workers had come to know better times, and youth was not doing badly in the schools. The Ukrainians seemed to be making progress everywhere except in business. While the Ukrainian immigrant was becoming hunchbacked from hard work, Jewish merchants, for example, were getting fat on the Ukrainian settlements.

Out of habit, the Ukrainian woman who shopped in Jewish stores in the Old Country continued the same practice in Canada. Because the idea had never appealed to them before, the settlers felt no need to run their own stores. Both in the Old Country and in Canada, they left that role to foreigners. They also feared bankruptcy. They did not believe the Ukrainian woman would shop at a store run by a Ukrainian rather than, for example, a Jew.

The first Ukrainian who dared go into business was Paul Rudyk, a native of Lishnyv, Brody County, Galicia. He came to Canada in 1897 with his parents, who settled at Beaver Lake, Alberta. By 1901 he lived in Edmonton, where he acted as an interpreter for the newcomers in English stores. Later he opened his own little store on Kinistino [96th] Street and was involved in real estate. He even put foreigners to shame with his drive, hard work and business sense.

By 1911 he was considered the richest Ukrainian in Canada. In 1912 he managed the International Hotel and owned the four-storey Rudyk Block on Jasper Avenue.

Another Ukrainian who went into business soon after he arrived was Fedor Farion of Borshchiv County, who settled in Sifton, Manitoba. In 1904 he opened a small store in a little shack and within a few years had a general store with various goods and a steam-operated mill called the Farion Milling Company.

We are not sure who was the first Ukrainian to go into business in Saskatchewan. It is said that Vasyl Katarynych of Hafford was an able businessman and one of the first. He was involved in grain and hotels but soon disappeared from the commercial scene. He owned the Hafford Hotel and was probably the first Ukrainian after Paul Rudyk to venture into that profitable business.

We will not dwell on how Ukrainian young people got into business, because they entered in different ways and for different reasons. Some were simply attracted to it; others were envious of the Jewish merchants who made money off the Ukrainians and wished to do the same. Still others got fed up with working on the railroad or in the mines and, having saved some money, decided to try to earn an easier living. As well, many of the first Ukrainian-English teachers, not fortunate enough to attend university, tried business after they got tired of teaching. By the time these recollections were written, some three thousand Ukrainians were engaged in the retail trade, in addition to skilled tradesmen and professionals.

The following story by Nykolai Virsta of Bellis, Alberta, illustrates how a typical Ukrainian worker got himself established:

My Experiences in Canada

At home in the Old Country there were nine of us in the family—five boys and four girls, but my oldest brother died when he was seven, so there were eight of us left. My parents were poor. They started out with only one and a half morgen of land, but through hard work they owned fourteen morgen by their old age. The children helped them.

When I was sixteen I went to work on the landowner's field, swinging the scythe like a grown man. As a small boy I went to school, but a child exhausted by domestic chores doesn't do well in school. I had barely finished grade three when my parents asked the priests and the principal to let me go because there was hard work in the household.

They did. It was common at the time for the older people to worry more about earning a living than about school.

In 1907 I was drafted into the army. I served in the Thirtieth Artillery Regiment stationed at Pekulychi, near Peremyshl in Galicia. At first it had its ups and downs but when I got used to it, it wasn't so bad. In 1909 I was transferred to Vienna for four months and then to Prague for two. I learned a lot in those countries, including German. In 1910 I was sent back to my regiment in Peremyshl, where I asked the commanding officer for a two-week furlough to visit my folks in Perehynska in Dolyna County. They let me go.

While I was in the army, four fellows from our village had emigrated to Canada, though they called it America. I went to their families in the village and read their letters from America. The letters said that everything was fine, that they were earning fifteen crowns a day and had already sent some money to their parents. I went home and told my parents that I also wanted to go to America, right away. My father didn't agree, and said, "You're a soldier, son. You can't desert. If they catch you, you'll pay for it." I replied that it was a waste of time to spend another eight months in the army. My brother supported me and my father gave in after asking, "What'll you do with your uniform and your sword?"

"I'll send them back to the regiment."

That same day I wrote to the steamship agents for information, and in a few days I got their reply. I went to the reeve, whom I knew well, and asked him to issue a work permit for Germany, which he did. I was at home for eight days, then my father took me to the railway station at Krekhovychi, where we said good-bye. We kissed each other and he cried because he felt he would never see me again. Before I boarded the train he reminded me to behave myself in Canada, to respect others, to be frugal, not to forget my brothers and sisters and not to forget my faith or to abandon my religion.

I arrived at Peremyshl in the evening and was tempted to say hello to my buddies at the station, but I was afraid to leave the car in case someone recognized me in civilian clothes. Through the window I spotted my very good friend, Sergeant Orzhechovsky, but didn't show myself to him because I was scared stiff that someone would find out I was a deserter.

We came to Myslowits, where there was passport inspection. With me was my young cousin, Petro Luklan, who was also going to Germany on a work permit. The inspectors immediately began to separate the passengers according to their destination, and we got to Germany successfully. There I began to breathe easier because I was sure that we would not be turned back. By 6 March we were on our way to Antwerp, where we waited two days for a ship. We wandered around the city gawking at the tall buildings and beautiful churches. By

9 March we were at sea on a freighter that had brought cattle from Canada to Europe. We slept on iron bunkbeds with over two hundred of us in one compartment. The agents had said that there were all kinds of conveniences on the ship and that it was a mail clipper with four funnels, yet here we were living in the same space previously occupied by cattle. They had simply whitewashed it with lime or something to get rid of the animal odour.

On 21 March we arrived at St. John and then sailed to Quebec, where again we were inspected for sickness. People had been very sick and the food was bad. They had given us a lot of fish, which just made people sicker. For this inspection, each passenger was supposed to have twenty-five dollars cash; otherwise they said he'd be sent back. I was terrified because I had only fifteen dollars, but in a tight corner a man learns quickly. I folded the ten-dollar bill in two with the corners up and, when passing the official, showed him I had twenty-five. When I got through this I felt like a lucky man. Now that I'm in Canada, I thought, all my problems will be over. In a couple of hours we boarded a train and headed west. We travelled over the Ontario wilderness till we got sick of it. On the third day, about evening, we arrived in Winnipeg.

At some small station before Winnipeg we recognized Fedor Iatsuka from the Old Country. He had been looking for a job, but since there wasn't anything, he was returning to Winnipeg. We were very glad to have run across him because we knew he could help us. The first night all three of us slept on a single mattress because there was no bed in his room. The next day we went into town to get something to eat and to look around for work, but we couldn't find any. On the third day, while looking for work, we came across a group of people standing in front of an office. We heard them speaking Ukrainian, so we asked what they were waiting for and were told that people were being signed up for work. We asked what kind of work and were told that it was excavating and hauling earth with mules. The pay was thirty-five dollars a month with board. That's a pile of money, I thought. You couldn't make that much money in the Old Country in half a year. We signed up too.

Early the next day we took a train and by evening were in a small place called Balcarres, Saskatchewan. From the station we walked two miles to a farm where there were all kinds of wagons, ploughs, scrapers and other machinery, as well as many horses and mules. This was D. G. McArthur's ranch. He was the main contractor for new roads and railways. The next day we got down to work. We packed up the tents, loaded the wagons and, like the Tatars of old, headed further west across the steppes. We went about eighteen miles and camped near what seemed to be a nice river. But it was full of snakes swimming around like fish. I saw nothing like it before or since.

There we began to construct a bed for the railway track. Some

excavated and others moved earth with big scrapers called "Fresnoes."
A man with four horses or mules was paid forty dollars a month. The
work was tough but the money was good. We worked eight months, till
freeze-up. From there I sent my parents sixty dollars and later another
forty when I got back to Winnipeg.

In the winter I signed up for bush work at Fort Frances, Ontario, at
twenty dollars a month. I barely lasted a month. It was a hard winter,
extremely cold with deep snow. I couldn't put up with the hard work. It
was eighteen miles to the station and I was on foot, but luckily I came
across a stove-heated water tank by the track, where I warmed up a bit
and made it to the station. A train came by in a couple of hours and I
returned to Winnipeg. At that time workingmen wandered from station
to station with bags over their shoulders like beggars in the Old
Country. Without money, one had to walk, hungry and cold, sometimes
for hundreds of miles. Eventually all passes and is forgotten.

In Winnipeg I got a job on an "extra" gang at $1.25 per day, out of
which I had to pay board. It was hard work, but we had to do it to live.
I worked a full month. I had always wanted to get to the mines in
British Columbia and at last, in the spring of 1911, men were being
taken on a new road near Edson, Alberta. The pay was two dollars a
day, with a dollar off for board.

From Winnipeg we went on the CNR to Edmonton, then Edson.
From Edson to Hinton the train went along at five to ten miles an hour
because the road bed was flooded and there was a lot of debris. The
train swayed like a ship. It was terrifying. It seemed like it might fall
over or jump the track. From Hinton we walked for two days till we
came to our camp, with the tents all set up and much equipment ready
to go. This was the Grand Trunk Railroad.

We picked up our hoes, picks, shovels and axes and began cutting
down the trees and clearing the bush on the right of way. The earth was
still frozen and the foreman was some Scotchman [*sic*] who never
stopped swearing. We worked there for two days and fled. On the way
back we ran across another road gang whose foreman hired us. He was
a kind man and we worked for him till fall.

In the winter of 1912 I signed up in Edmonton for bush work west of
Edson and worked there two months for nothing because the contractor
went bankrupt. Hungry, I barely made it back to Edmonton and found
some kind of boarding house on 96th Street. It cost twenty dollars a
month, but I didn't have a cent. For three days I hunted for a job in
and around Edmonton till I finally found one in a brick factory and
made just enough to pay the lady of the house for board.

In the spring I again went to Hinton to work on the railroad, where I
stayed till fall. In the winter I signed up again for bush work, this time
in Prince Albert, Saskatchewan. I didn't work there long because I got
very sick and came back to Edmonton. In 1913 I worked at a variety of

jobs and for the winter of 1914 went to Brew Lake to cut railway ties. There I learned of a new coal mine that was being opened up and got a job. We drilled a tunnel to the coal face, blasting with dynamite day and night. It was very dangerous work, but we had to work to survive.

Even after we got to the coal, the work was hard because there was no fresh air until we broke through to the surface. By this time most of the men had left, so I had nothing to do but to go back to Edmonton. Then war broke out between Austria and Serbia and all foreigners had to register. Ivan Ivanytsky and I both got jobs in Edmonton at the Western Steel Company. We worked for three months and then were laid off, probably because we were foreigners. We went to Delph, Alberta, where we worked for fifty cents a day threshing at Mykhailo Tychkovsky's and Vasyl Fedyniak's. We stayed with them that winter and I taught their children Ukrainian for which I was paid fifty cents a month per child.

In 1915 I went back to Brew Lake and got a job in a mine. The pit boss was Mr. Blake, followed by Mr. Currie, a very smart man under whom the work went well. I worked there a year and a half. I made some money and with two others rented a hall in the Rudyk Block to show moving pictures. We didn't stay in that business for long because the rent was high and the films expensive. With the admission five cents, it just didn't pay. In a month we closed down and Dmytro Halushko and I went to Yellowhead, to the coal mine near the Coal Spur Branch, where I almost lost my life in a cave-in. From there I went to Corbin, B. C., and then worked in Big Show, Blairmore and Rossdale. In 1918 I returned to Coal Spur and then to the Cadomin mine.

In 1919 the war was over and I received a letter from the Old Country that things were worse [under Poland] than they had been under Austria, so I decided to stay in Canada. In the small town of Cadomin I built myself a shack and decided to get married. I married Vasyl Kutrya's daughter from Chipman. In 1920 the Cadomin mine caught fire and fifty of us miners fought the fire for a month and failed to put it out. It was like hell. We worked for sixteen hours a day with death threatening us every minute. Many left until there were only about a dozen who wanted to earn some money. We opened a shaft on the other side of the mountain and began mining coal.

In December my wife got sick and the Cadomin doctor treated her for a whole year, but nothing helped. I took her to Edmonton to see Dr. Allan who operated on her, but the next day, that is, 1 January 1919, she died at the Royal Alexandra Hospital.

After all these troubles I lost interest in my job. Although I kept working, it all seemed pointless. In mid-July I took a holiday, as they say, and went to Toronto. There I met some Ukrainians, including Mariia, a former neighbour of mine from my native village, the daugher of Mykhailo and Anna Melnyk of the Luklan family. In December we returned to Edmonton, where we got married. After a couple of days, I left my wife with some good folks in Edmonton and went to the coal mine to earn some money. But it so happened that the miners went out on strike and there wasn't any work till June. I brought my wife out, and while I crawled around in the tunnels digging coal with the miners, she cooked and washed for us.

In 1925 I was injured in the mine so badly that I couldn't stand on my feet and ever since I've had problems with my legs. That year we left the mine and went to Bellis where we bought a building that was called a "hotel." It cost us a lot of work and money before we made it into a real hotel. In 1925 the government gave us a licence to sell beer and to rent rooms. Two years later I joined in the partnership that owned the flour mill in Bellis. Business wasn't too bad in both the hotel and the mill, but when the hotel burned down, and then the mill, we lost more than $8,000. We then built another hotel.

I lived through a lot of things in those thirty-two years, but you couldn't list them all on an ox's hide. It wasn't I alone who lived through hard times; the experience of thousands was even worse. When you look back, you wonder just how a human being could put up with it all. Anyway, it's nice to think about those years because they're like a dream. They came and went like a dream-like odyssey.

Ukrainians and Canadian Politics

Not every citizen of a given country is equally interested in social issues and national affairs. Much depends on the system of government, the awareness of its citizens and the national organizations and their leaders.

When Ukrainians first settled Canada, it was still an ordinary colony though it had a form of self-government. Western Canada, in particular, was not organized for self-government. It was a colony and its political system reflected that circumstance.

When a Ukrainian colonist arrived in this vast country and settled far in the wilderness, governmental and political systems did not interest him. He knew his job was homesteading—cutting down trees, pulling stumps, clearing boulders out of the ground and building a farm. Having done that, he would get his patent, a form of recognition, something like a reward or a medal for pioneer "heroism."

To get his patent, the colonist had also to sign a declaration swearing allegiance to queen or king and country. He would then receive his naturalization certificate and become a citizen of Canada, but not of Great Britain.

When it came time for federal, provincial or local elections, political hucksters visited the new citizens and taught them how and for whom to vote. It would happen that such an agent would visit a farmer in the morning and tell him to vote for Harrison because he was a fine man, while in the evening another agent would come and say that Mr. Harrison was a so-and-so and that all Ukrainians should vote for Ferguson because his party brought the Ukrainians to Canada.

Often during a federal election people would get citizenship papers if they promised the agent they would vote for his party, which had the power to issue them. Although it was illegal, the agent had this power and nobody else. Sometimes they were nothing but empty promises. Those who were illiterate had the most problems. Some would get the patent to their land but not their citizenship papers.

Among the Ukrainians who first took an interest in politics in their community were Theodore Stefanyk, Mykhailo Sloboda, Tomko Yastremsky [Iastremsky], M. Dyma, Ivan Negrich, Vasyl Karakotsiuk, Paul Gigeychuk, T. D. Ferley, Fedia Tatsiuk and Vasyl Tsiupak, all of Winnipeg. Besides these, there were local politicians in the settlements who played leading roles during the elections.

In Saskatchewan the following were interested in politics: P. Shvydky, Ivan Puhaty, Mykhailo Kun, M. Ostrovsky, J. Megas, Iu. Androchowicz and numerous others. In Alberta those considered to be pioneer politicians were P. Killyar, Paul Rudyk, Michael Gowda, Peter Svarich, Andrew Shandro, Vasyl Pillipiw, Theodore Nemirsky, Peter [Petro] Kulmatytsky, Kindrat Sheremeta and others.

When Ukrainians first came to Canada, there were only two political parties in the country, so you voted for one or the other. At times it was whose bottle of whisky sat on the table that told you who won the election. They even joked, "What's the difference: one costs eighteen cents and the other twenty minus two."

Ukrainians took politics more seriously when they understood English better, learned to read and write and began to feel more at home—and most of all when they realized that all that is good in a country comes from its people and their concern and all that is bad results from their apathy and neglect.

The First Ukrainian MLA in Alberta

When the Ukrainian immigrant got used to the new language, grew more knowledgeable about this rich land's customs and leaders, and became aware that he too was a citizen because he cleared the land of bush, pulled stumps and roots from the ground, ploughed it and sowed golden wheat, built roads, farms, public buildings, schools, towns and villages—then and only then, in full comprehension of his citizenship, did he take an interest in local politics. Some tried to become school trustees and others district councillors and reeves of municipalities. They actively participated in everything, but they did not have the courage to run for the Legislature. They thought that perhaps they were not wealthy enough or sufficiently experienced.

The first Ukrainian who dared to run for federal Parliament was Vasyl Holovatsky, a socialist. He lived in Winnipeg and ran in the Selkirk constituency in Manitoba. He got 146 votes. He was pushed into the whirlwind of politics by Paul Crath and Matthew Popovich [Matvii Popovych], organizers of the international socialist movement among Ukrainian workers in Winnipeg and beyond.

Their socialist paper was in danger of bankruptcy, so they decided to enter politics because it was possible to raise money during an election campaign for political propaganda and still have some left over on the side. Later they would often repeat this practice, even though they were sure their candidate had no chance.

After his electoral attempt, V. Holovatsky got angry at his comrades and left them to join a religious sect known as the Russellites, for whom he preached the Bible in the United States, where he died. Four years later Paul Crath also left the internationalists and in 1915 was ordained a Presbyterian minister in Toronto.

Out of the trio, only Matthew Popovich was left holding the fort, but he was somewhat estranged from the Ukrainian community because he had married a Jewish woman. His brothers-in-law helped him promote internationalism among the unenlightened central European peoples.

A decisive and real political movement, worthy of the name, began among the early settlers in Alberta in 1913. In mid-January, the Alberta Legislature was dissolved and a new election called for 21 April. Prominent Ukrainians like Roman Kremar, Paul Rudyk,

Peter Svarich and others decided it was time for Ukrainians to get actively involved. After the redistribution of electoral boundaries, it looked as if the Ukrainians, with some effort and solid organization, might be able to elect at least three members to the Legislature. Why not nominate Ukrainian candidates? Kremar suggested a general meeting, which was held in Chipman at the beginning of February.*

Ukrainians lived in the following electoral districts: Victoria with the town of Lamont its centre; Whitford with Shandro its centre; Vegreville with Vegreville its centre; Vermilion, which went as far north as the North Saskatchewan River and had Manville as its centre; and Sturgeon with Egremont its centre. There were other districts where Ukrainians lived but in smaller numbers. The largest percentage lived in the Whitford electoral district. There was a real hope that even if their man was not elected elsewhere, he would certainly get in there. And that is just what happened.

The rally at Chipman attracted people from the farthest corners of the several settlements. Some people drove their horses for two days to get there. It was the first public rally. The speakers delivered impassioned and patriotic speeches that made an impact on the audience. They stressed that the voters should try to nominate their own people during district nominating meetings.

When someone in the audience asked the chairman whether the party would accept the Ukrainian candidates, there was an uproar and everyone turned in the direction of the questioner. The issue of what the party would say drove a wedge into the whole affair. Those who had experience in elections quickly went outside and began discussions among themselves. The party in question was the Liberal party, in power in Alberta at the time, and the vast majority of the voters at the rally were committed supporters of the Liberal party.

Some of the organizers of the meeting realized that nothing was going to happen, so they put on their sheepskin coats and went home. Those who remained were the ones who wanted to have their cake and eat it too. They therefore decided to send a resolution

---

* For evidence that the meeting was on 14 January in Vegreville, see *Kanadyiskyi rusyn* (Canadian Ruthenian), 4 January, 15 February 1913. (Ed.)

from the rally to Premier Sifton in Edmonton expressing their wishes and sentiments.

The resolution, reprinted here in full, appeared in the *Edmonton Bulletin* [12 March 1913] under the following heading:

February, 1913

RUTHENIANS ARE WITH GOVERNMENT

Large Gathering Held at Chipman at Which Resolution Approving the Sifton Administration is Unanimously Passed.

A delegation of Ruthenians waited on Premier Sifton a few days ago and presented him with a copy of the following resolution, which was passed at a large gathering of Ruthenian delegates held at Chipman:

Resolved, That we convey to the Honorable A. L. Sifton, Premier of Alberta, our high regard for and confidence in him, and for his Government and the private members supporting him, in whose constituencies the majority of our people are his strong supporters.

That we bespeak from him and them, the same equitable treatment in the future that we have had in the past.

Resolved, That we appreciate the Franchise which is granted as freely to us as to any other people of foreign birth and in the exercise of that privilege and of the privilege of nomination as a political candidate, we do so as Canadian citizens.

Resolved, That, while we are proud of the country of our birth, and desire ever to keep before us its highest ideals, we recognize that in this, our adopted country, we as citizens are accorded all the rights and privileges of Canadian citizenship and that we believe it to be our duty to work in harmony with all our fellow citizens to build up a united and prosperous nation without distinction of race or creed.

We believe this to be not only our duty, but in the best interest of ourselves and our children, today and of future generations, who, we confidently believe, will be intimately associated with the social, commercial and political life of this great free country of our adoption.

Failure at the Nominating Meetings

At the mass meeting in Chipman there were Ukrainians from all walks of life and viewpoints, so it was impossible to satisfy them all. Every group wanted to nominate its own candidate but there was no room for that. It must not be forgotten that at the time Ukrainians in Alberta were seriously divided because of religious differences. Those who wanted to be candidates knew this and so were not brave enough to nominate themselves. Instead, they waited for the public rally to decide, which it did not do. Everyone therefore went home disappointed to await the official Liberal nominating meetings and to see which candidates would be chosen by the delegates. The only one who campaigned among the delegates was Andrew Shandro in Whitford district. Everyone else waited for the ready-made "*holubtsi*" [cabbage rolls].

Dissatisfied Electors

The delegates sent by the "people" to the official nominating meetings allowed themselves to be swayed, and once they saw this, the Ukrainian candidates did not even try to let their names stand for nomination. With the exception of Whitford, all the meetings nominated non-Ukrainians. This upset some electors who spread dissatisfaction among their neighbours. "The party likes Ukrainians when they support it," they said, "but when it comes to electing a Ukrainian to the Legislature, the party turns its back on them." Although in all honesty this accusation was groundless, some people listened to it.

Failing to nominate their own candidates at the Liberal conventions, the Vegreville district tried their luck at the Conservative convention held on 31 March in Vegreville. They launched an extensive advance campaign in the district, and with the majority of delegates of Ukrainian origin, they were certain they would succeed in nominating Peter Kulmatytsky of the Conservative party. On the day of the convention Vegreville was choked full of delegates and farmers from all over the district, full of hope that victory would be theirs.

The Town Hall auditorium was packed. When the curtain was raised, there sat Peter Kulmatytsky along with the rest of the Conservative party committee. The crowd burst into loud applause and Mr. Fraser, the president of the local Conservative Club, opened the convention.

The Ukrainian delegates looked round and rubbed their hands with glee when they saw that there were more of them than others. They were confident of victory, but the non-Ukrainians thought otherwise. The secretary read out the procedure according to which the convention and other party business would be conducted. Someone moved that a nominating committee be struck to consider the candidates and the motion carried. The Ukrainians supported it, not realizing that it was a political trick which allowed a majority of non-Ukrainians to slip onto the nominating committee.

While speakers spoke on various political topics, the nominating committee deliberated behind the curtain. In half an hour the committee chairman came to the rostrum and announced that the candidate for the Vegreville district was Mr. Morrison, a local lawyer.

The auditorium burst into pandemonium. The Ukrainians demanded an open vote, while the chairman tried to convince them that the nomination was legal. A. Zygmant, a delegate from Innisfree, sprang to the table, grabbed the register of the meeting and fled, with the secretary and B. Rodgers, the town constable, on his heels. The Ukrainians realized what was happening and rushed out to save Zygmant, with the crowd in pursuit. It was not long before fighting broke out among the delegates in the auditorium, in the corridor, out on the street and in the marketplace.

The "war" raged for almost an hour and even lunch barely appeased the participants. They patrolled the streets in small groups to watch for the enemy's approach. Zygmant hid till after lunch, and when he did show up, he threw the book at the constable, saying, "To h... with your book, we'll nominate our own candidate without it." And that is what happened.

Around two o'clock the dissatisfied delegates met at the marketplace and proposed that Peter Svarich accept the candidacy as an independent. He was there and immediately jumped onto a farmer's wagon and declared, "Up to now I've been a fervent supporter of the Liberal party, but in this campaign I've noticed that neither the Liberals nor the Conservatives treat Ukrainians as citizens, so I accept your nomination to be an independent candidate in the Vegreville district." The crowd burst into applause.

Michael Gowda agreed to run as an independent in Victoria and Hryhorii Kraikivsky in the Vermilion district, though both were once Liberals. Paul Rudyk ran as an Independent Liberal against Andrew Shandro, the government-approved candidate in Whitford, along with two English candidates, Dr. Connolly, an Independent Liberal, and Dick Houston, a Conservative. In Sturgeon, no Ukrainian dared run against the Minister of Education, J. R. Boyle. None of the independent Ukrainian candidates won a seat. Only Andrew Shandro was elected.

Provincial Elections and Ukrainian Teachers in Alberta

After the sensational Alberta election of 1913, the re-elected Minister of Education, J. R. Boyle, did not forget what the Ukrainians had cooked up for him and his party. In order to take revenge, he blamed a handful of what he called "Galician teachers" for being the political instigators behind the nomination of Ukrainian candidates. He was convinced of this by Mykhailo Ostrovsky, a Russophile from the Lemko district of Galicia and a Liberal party organizer among Ukrainians in the province.

It did not take more than a month after the election for Mr. Boyle to cancel, with a single stroke of his pen, the teaching permits of these "Galician teachers." There were three Ukrainian students from Alberta College—H. Gavinchuk, M. Goshko and P. Bozyk [Bozhyk]—teaching in Alberta, as well as seven students from Manitoba College in Winnipeg and likely three Ukrainian-English teachers with third class certificates from Manitoba. They were certainly all permit holders, because there was not a single qualified Ukrainian teacher in Alberta at the time. The first Ukrainian, Wasyl Kuriets, did not graduate from normal school in Alberta until 1916.

Mr. Boyle thought that by dismissing these teachers his troubles would be over. For the next four years at least, he would have peace and quiet and the Ukrainians would return to being docile sheep politically. It did not turn out that way. His "ukaze" infuriated the 'meek' Ukrainians. The whole Ukrainian community protested to such an extent that both Mr. Boyle and the Liberal party in Alberta suffered.

Ukrainians who had once zealously supported Liberal candidates during the elections stopped believing that the party which had always bragged about its liberalism and friendship toward them was in fact a freedom-loving party.

Trustees of the Kolomea, Stanislaviv and Bukowina Schools Go to Court

Mr. Boyle's "ukaze" enraged not only the taxpayers of the school districts where there were Ukrainian teachers, but almost the whole Ukrainian community. The Kolomea School District, where Ivan Genik, a second-year philosophy student from the University of Manitoba, was teaching, would not accept the English teacher brought by the official trustee, R. Fletcher. The taxpayers of Stanislaviv School, where J. J. Mykytiuk from Manitoba was teaching, did the same thing. As a result, they ended up in court, where they were fined and reminded that an order was an order.

The taxpayers of Bukowina School, where W. A. Czumer, a teacher from Manitoba, taught, did not resist but quietly and without complaining built a private school next to the public one. Czumer taught in that private school according to the provisions of the School Act. Not one child was sent to the public school to which R. Fletcher brought the "qualified" Alberta teacher.

The ingenuity and determination of the Bukovynians angered Mr. Boyle, nor was it good for the "Russian" MLA [Andrew Shandro] in whose district (almost at his doorstep) all this was happening.* Although the School Act allowed private schools in the province, opposing the minister's orders and building a private school where a public one already existed lowered his prestige. He could not accept the insult. Furthermore, the Conservative MLAs accused him of political intolerance and of behaving like a dictator.

To avoid the reproach of his party colleagues and to divert public opinion, he put all the blame on the "Russo-Galician" and "Bukovynian" teachers. The following is reprinted as it appeared in English in the Liberal newspaper, the *Edmonton Bulletin*, 20 August 1913:

CONTROL OF RUTHENIAN SCHOOLS IN ALBERTA MUST BE FIRMLY MAINTAINED

Vigorous Measures Adopted to Ensure English Education For Children of Foreign Parents

TEACHERS FROM MANITOBA SUMMARILY DISMISSED

Minister of Education Deals Firmly With Refractory Galician School Trustees

The department of education for Alberta has a real live problem on its hands in connection with the education of foreigners. The Galicians have been putting up a big fight to get control of the schools in their own districts and install Galician teachers. A number of Galicians who had been employed in Manitoba schools came here last spring and were at once installed by the Galician school boards.

---

* The term "Russian" stemmed from the prominence of the Russian Orthodox church in the Shandro district. (Ed.)

It is stated that many of these so-called teachers were scarcely able to speak and write English. When this condition of affairs was discovered by the department, Mr. Fletcher, the supervisor of schools among foreigners, was instructed to at once have properly qualified normal school trained teachers placed in these schools.

In a number of cases the foreign teacher refused to quit and as the Galician school board refused to dismiss him, the Hon. John R. Boyle, minister of education, appointed Mr. Fletcher as official trustee and he at once proceeded to dismiss the Galician untrained teacher and install the regular teacher.

SCHOOL TRUSTEES OBSTRUCT

The opposition raised was so strong in the Kolomea and Bukowina school districts that it was necessary to have the school trustees brought before a magistrate and fined for interfering with the qualified teacher in the discharge of his duties. In the case of the Bukowina school district the parents of the children have now decided not to send their children to school.

The Hon. J. R. Boyle, minister of education, interviewed on the subject today, stated that if these Galicians continued to absent their children from school the Truancy Act would be put into force against them. Mr. Fletcher is meanwhile acting as official trustee and he sees to it that the district pays the salary of the properly qualified teacher.

STRONG MEASURES NECESSARY

In Manitoba the Galicians were allowed to get control of their schools with the result that the children are growing up in the province unable to speak a word of English. Mr. Boyle emphatically declared that no such state of affairs would be permitted in Alberta.

"This is an English speaking province," said Mr. Boyle, "and every Alberta boy and girl should receive a sound English education in the public schools of the province."

Mr. Boyle added that there appeared to be an active organization among the Galicians to acquire control of the schools and have them conducted by Galician teachers in their own language. It was evident that strong measures on the part of the department of education would be required to keep control of the situation in the foreign settled districts.

NO FAVORITISM

"The policy of conducting the schools by teachers speaking the English language and teaching in English with no favoritism in the matter of teachers certificates, is one that should appeal to the people of Alberta as a sound educational policy and should have the support of the great majority of people in the province."

Novyny Reacts

The Ukrainian newspaper, *Novyny*, which was then published in Edmonton, wrote the following response on 22 August to the *Bulletin*'s article on "Galician Schools":

THE LIBERALS DECLARE WAR ON UKRAINIANS

Government Organs in Edmonton [the **Capital** *and the* **Bulletin***] Threaten To Deprive Ukrainians of the Right to Run Their Own Schools.*

SHAMEFUL LIES BY THE MINISTER OF EDUCATION
SPECIAL LAWS AGAINST UKRAINAN PEOPLE

Liberal Gratitude

Ukrainian Albertans, this, in black and white, is the gratitude of the Liberal party for your long and loyal support. This is the proof of how fond the government is of you; the same government that won the last provincial election with your votes. This is how the promises made to you by the Siftons, the Boyles, the Olivers and the rest of the Liberal higher-ups are fulfilled. As they say, "What is sealed with a pen cannot be freed with an ox." This is precise proof of the Liberal party's "love" for Ukrainians, which it can never wipe out with sweet talk and promises.

The Liberal party started a wild and shameless witch hunt for "loyal" Ukrainians. The lies and insults directed at Ukrainians did not come from some irresponsible person but from the minister of education himself, whose words the *Bulletin* underlines and for whom you voted in the Sturgeon riding.

From the fact that both Liberal dailies in Edmonton took the same stand against Ukrainians, we can assume that the whole Liberal party under the leadership of Premier Sifton, the same Sifton whom Ukrainians elected with their votes in Vermilion, has declared war on the Ukrainian people in a life-and-death struggle, as the articles below indicate:

Impertinent Pretensions

"THIS IS AN ENGLISH PROVINCE," cries Boyle, "AND EVERY BOY AND GIRL IN ALBERTA MUST RECEIVE AN ENGLISH EDUCATION."

The scatter-brained editor of the *Bulletin* himself uncovers nothing less horrible than "GALICIANS PREPARING A BIG BATTLE TO WIN CONTROL OF SCHOOLS IN THEIR DISTRICTS." Can there be anything more monstrous than a man wanting to be master in his OWN home?

Alberta Liberals consider any Ukrainian who catches Mr. Boyle in his pantry or Mr. Fletcher in his stable to be a thief. Because this is an English province, Mr. Boyle has a right to steal anything he likes from a Ukrainian pantry and Mr. Fletcher has a right to lead out the best horses from a Ukrainian stable whenever they want to because they are English. Can this degenerate logic sink any further?

Fortunately, we still have enough respect for the truly cultured Englishman not to conclude from the stupid statements of a foolish minister and editor that all Englishmen share the cutthroat pretensions of Alberta Liberal ministers and editors.

We know very well the English proverb, "My home is my castle," and we know that if an Englishman caught an uninvited guest in his pantry or stable, he would not wait for a court hearing but would settle the matter in a quicker way just as would a Ukrainian.

A school built by the community for itself is the property of the community, and all ministers should learn to keep their hands off of it. Mr. Boyle has no more right to interfere with it than he has to crawl into someone else's pantry.

The basic right of the Canadian constitution is the self-government of its citizens and not the despotism of political adventurists. Laws passed by the Alberta Legislature are proof of how schools are to be run in the province. Neither the minister of education nor all the ministers put together have the right to enact a new law or do away with an existing one. For an official to tamper with the law is the worst crime that can be committed in a constitutional country.

Boyle, Alberta's minister of education, must be either a simpleton who does not know the laws of Alberta or a criminal who violates the Canadian constitution.

The Minister Lies

The minister of education lies when he appeals to the egoism of English jingoists with words that can be interpreted to mean that all languages except English are forbidden in Alberta schools. Paragraph 139 of the School Act states that any other language which the parents wish can be taught in public schools.

The minister of education lies when he says that Alberta is an English province. Alberta is a Canadian province, where everyone has equal rights, including the Ukrainians, who in percentage terms comprise one of the largest nationalities in the province. Not to know this is the height of ignorance, which would disqualify the minister from holding even the post of a mounted policeman in the province.

Furthermore, the minister of education is a shameless and base liar when he claims that the teachers from Manitoba cannot speak English. Perhaps only the Biblical Ananias could lie so brazenly. The minister cites two examples of school districts from which the heroic Fletcher dismissed "uneducated teachers"—Kolomea and Bukowina. Who were these teachers? In Kolomea it was Mr. Ivan Genyk, a second-year student of philosophy at the University of Manitoba. In Bukowina it was Mr. William Czumer with a teacher's diploma from Manitoba. Mr. Czumer completed his training in Winnipeg with honours and has been teaching continually for the past six years in public schools to the general satisfaction of the ministry of education, all school inspectors and members of the community. On what basis does Boyle have a right to claim that a teacher who passed his examinations long ago and a university student are unable to speak English? Really, one has to have the face of a prostitute to say something like this to the English public without being ashamed.

"Galician"

We simply fail to understand why Mr. Boyle, the *Bulletin* and the *Capital* took this specific opportunity to dredge up the word "Galician." To accuse the minister of ignorance of the fact that nowhere in the world is there a "Galician" nationality would be tantamount to insulting all cultured Englishmen who live in this province, because even cowboys and swineherds, much less the minister, know by now that there is no such thing as a "Galician" language or nationality. There are only Ukrainians, Poles, Germans, Jews and other nationalities from a province in Austria called Galicia, who have nothing in common except a deep hatred for each other; there is also a province in Spain called Galicia with which Ukrainians are not connected.

To further accuse the minister of education for Alberta of wanting, out of frustration and anger, to revenge himself on Ukrainians by calling them "Galicians" (a term used in the street by common ordinary ruffians) would also be an insult to Englishmen for putting such a man in the minister's chair. Let the world judge him by his deeds.

But we cannot stop here; we have accused Boyle of overstepping the Canadian constitution.

Without Any Right

That Boyle or Fletcher asked the teachers to resign is a fabrication. Fletcher brought English teachers to the Ukrainian settlements and dismissed the Ukrainian teachers outright, without any formalities, like a typical henchman from the ranks of the Department of Education. We can prove this in court.

Nobody informed the citizens that the Department of Education disapproved of Ukrainian teachers. On the contrary, school inspectors praised the dismissed teachers for their good work in the schools. Fletcher descended on the colony unexpectedly and immediately brought new teachers with him. He encountered resistance only when the trustees defended their constitutional rights. No one notified them that they were suspended from doing their duty, or that steps were being taken in that direction, or that a general official trustee for all of Alberta, named Fletcher, had been appointed over them. The minister of education provoked the Ukrainian settlers, and it must be considered a miracle that Fletcher was not lynched. It is certain that if one acted in such a provocative manner toward the English, they would not let him out of their colony alive.

Who gave Boyle the right to appoint an official trustee? On what grounds? Let Boyle answer the question himself and then let him appeal to public opinion for sympathy.

We Want to Learn

Ukrainians did not protest in the past and do not protest now against the English language. Ukrainians want to know English, and the more the better. Ukrainians would be the first to dismiss from their colony any teacher who was unable to speak English. If they want Ukrainian teachers in their schools, it is only because the best English pedagogue cannot teach anything to a child who cannot understand him and with whom he must converse in sign language. For ten years English teachers sent by Boyle taught in the Bukowina School, and what came of their teaching? Not one child knew or understood English, and when a child read from a book he read mechanically without any comprehension. The true beginning of their knowledge of the English language was launched by Mr. Czumer. Now the children not only understand what they read, but they also can count and so on. The only result of the education given by the English teacher was that the children "read." Perhaps the teacher had the best of intentions originally, but finally he had to throw up his hands in despair and just be glad to be paid. And now, it seems, Fletcher's main problem is to see his darlings are appointed and get their pay, contrary to the taxpayer's wishes. Why else would the *Bulletin* make this a fact of such importance?

Afraid of His Own Shadow

Mr. Boyle should not think that this questioning of his statement that "favoritism plays no part here" is just a gentle hint. Boyle was lying shamelessly when he said this and he knew he was lying. We are prepared to supply witnesses who heard him say, "We are keeping Alberta schools for our friends." Those who understand the political machinations of the Alberta Liberals will need no explanation of who these "friends" are and why the Manitoba teachers have found themselves classed as enemies. That is where the bone is buried. It is not a question of English that concerns the minister of education but the political interests of the Liberal party.

The Pinnacle of Shamelessness

Finally, the limitless gall of this Liberal politician is visible in his tactic regarding the Manitoba school system. The Alberta minister of education dares to assert that in Manitoba, where "Galicians" control the schools, children are growing up without knowing a word of English. The only worthy response to a man who employs such arguments is to spit in his face, because a sober man would not say anything of the kind.

Empty Threats

For those who are interested we draw attention to what the [Truancy] Act says about neglected children, who are threatened by Alberta's half-baked minister of education.

Chapter 8

The Act Regarding Neglected Children and Compulsory Education is as Follows:

3. Every child who has attained the age of seven years and who has not yet attained the full age of fourteen years shall attend school for the full term during which the school of the district in which he resides is open each year, unless excused for the reasons hereinafter mentioned.

2. (d) By "school" is meant any public, separate or private school in which reading, writing, English literature, English grammar, geography and arithmetic are taught regularly.

Bukowina School

The Bukowina School was a private school in which teaching was conducted according to these paragraphs. So when Fletcher comes around or any other henchman appointed by the minister of education, you can whistle at him all you want and in case of any incident in this or any other school district, write immediately or come in person for advice to the editor of *Novyny*. Let Mr. Boyle teach flies in our colonies or, better still, let him attend school for a year himself to become a bit civilized because he is far from being a man.

The Vegreville Observer Defends Mr. Boyle

During and after the provincial election of 1913, the *Vegreville Observer*, a Liberal weekly, tried to defend Boyle's policy in connection with the problems he created in the Ukrainian school districts by placing all the blame on the loyal Ukrainian teachers, accusing them of separatism, as did the *Edmonton Bulletin*. One of its articles, published on 10 September 1913, is reprinted here in its entirety in English:

TAKING THE LID OFF

A Prominent Ruthenian Discloses Some of the Inside Working of the Alleged Protest Against English Teachers

The Observer has surely contrived to get into the middle of a warm controversy respecting the so-called Ruthenian schools. Now we are in it, however, we we will stay in it to the bitter end. As it is the only newspaper published within this district, so largely settled by Ruthenians, the Observer is naturally used as the vehicle of expression, both by those favoring the employment of Ruthenian teachers and by those who take the opposite view. In so far as the use of space is concerned both sides look alike to us, and we will cheerfully give any reasonable amount of space to those who wish to discuss this matter with moderation, and to contribute light rather than heat to the debate.

The following statement was made to the Observer by a well-known Ruthenian this week. It discloses some few things hitherto more or less unknown to the public generally:

The attitude of the Alberta Department of Education toward Ruthenian teachers had called out in Ruthenian papers as well as in some English Conservative papers a vigorous campaign against the head of the Department and many of the officials as well. In the Ruthenian weeklies this campaign is directed against all English speaking people and they are the victims of such terms as "bums," "cowboys," "fools," etc. These may be seen in copies of the Nowyny and the Canadian Ruthenian. These papers are also endeavoring to excite the entire Ruthenian settlement against the Department for its supposed unfavorable treatment of them. For that reason the Ruthenian patriots are asked to attend meetings in their districts to protest against the Department.

To understand the situation we have to go back to the 14th of January, 1913, when a Ruthenian mass meeting was held in Vegreville with the idea of establishing a Ruthenian Independent Political Party in Alberta. The idea was brought up by R. Kramar [*sic*] and Paul Rudyk after they had taken a trip to Winnipeg and had conversed with Manitoba politicians. At that famous meeting the Ruthenian Liberals (like Svarich, Shandro, Gowda, Fujarchuk, etc.) were nearly terrorized into withdrawing themselves from the Liberal party and joining the one which stood for Ruthenian National demands.

And what are these demands:

Mr. Kramar, in placing them before Hon. Mr. Boyle, demanded among other impossibilities, even a "Ruthenian University for Alberta."

The intention was to lay before the Minister conditions which they knew would not be acceptable, than [*sic*] after being refused, (which they knew would happen), they could attract the notice of the Ruthenian public to the Conservative party, on the grounds that they had assurance if the Conservatives were in power in Alberta, all Ruthenian demands would be satisfied. Immediately after that delegation waited on the Minister, the Conservatives started a Ruthenian weekly, "Nowyny," under the management of the said Mr. Kramar. The Board directing the so-called Ruthenian Independent Party also nominated at the same time five Ruthenian Independent candidates, in the hope only, that their candidates would draw all Ruthenian votes, and in that way assure the election of the Conservative candidates. For the election campaign they brought up from Manitoba prominent Conservative Ruthenian leaders, Messrs. Ferley, Czumer, Kuminsky, etc., to help Conservatives to be elected through work done for the Independent Ruthenian candidates. At the same time all the Ruthenian papers commenced an agitation to excite their countrymen against everything which is not Ruthenian. How well their work was done was shown in that famous free-for-all fight in Vegreville on March 31st.

In all these disturbances the Ruthenian teachers were taking the lead. After the election many of them remained in Alberta in order to prolong their Conservative and separatist activities. These Ruthenian teachers have only one idea, and that is to instruct the children and parents that as they were persecuted in Galicia by Polaks, in Russia by Russians, so they are persecuted in Canada by English fanatics; at election time their idea is to work against the Government. We all saw teachers Czumer, Sytnik, Bozik, Mykytiuk, etc., on the platforms at Vegreville and Mundare talking to the people and telling them that "the rule of English cowboys is finished; we are now in charge; we are a nation able to govern our own matters, etc."

To these political extravagances may be added that many of these Ruthenian teachers are unable to speak English. For instance, E. Kozlowsky, teacher of Podole school, in laying information before Magistrate Pozer, had to do so through the interpreter, Mr. Hestrin. Further it is well-known that in many instances the Ruthenian teachers left their class rooms after the Inspector, Mr. Butchart, came in. And they left these class rooms only for the reason that they could not converse with him in English.

Matters of this kind led the Department to look into it and take serious steps against a policy producing such results. There was another reason in that all these teachers were working under permits only; not one had the legal qualifications.

A Memorial to the First Ukrainian MLA in Alberta

All Ukrainians in Canada rejoiced when Andrew Shandro was elected to the Alberta Legislature in 1913, even though he himself then did not admit to being a Ukrainian. The Russian priests who served the Bukovynian Orthodox congregations took the most pride in him, along with all contemporary "Russophiles" of whom there were plenty in Alberta at the time.* They called a big rally on 12 July 1913 at the churchyard in Shandro, where they blessed a "memorial" in honour of the first "Russian" member of the Legislature in Alberta.

Many people from neighbouring Ukrainian settlements came. There were over three thousand, not counting the children. There were both Orthodox Bukovynians and Greek Catholics from Galicia. There was no lack of English Protestants from the Whitford district and even a few Liberal MLAs from Edmonton. It was a fine day that promised a grand celebration of both the holy day of Saints Peter and Paul and the triumph of Ukrainians in Alberta, who for the first time had elected their own man to the Legislature. Czumer, the Ukrainian-English teacher from the Bukowina School, led columns of his pupils to the church, even though R. Fletcher, the official trustee, had a day earlier brought a letter from the Department of Education to the local trustees instructing them to dismiss Czumer from their school and accept an Alberta "qualified" teacher in his place. The arrival of Czumer and his school children in Shandro evoked an unusual interest from those present, because the first "Russian" MLA did not expect such an accolade from Bukowina.

During his sermon the local Byelorussian priest, Reverend Pichinsky, praised the teacher: "My dear citizens! See what it means to have your own teacher. Did you ever see an English teacher, male or female, bringing children to your church?" His few words made such an impression on those present that even outsiders who were at the rally talked about it for a long time thereafter.

Following the church service and the dedication of the "memorial," and right after the dinner, a rally was held, chaired by Mykhailo Ostrovsky, the Liberal organizer among Ukrainians in Alberta mentioned earlier.

The first speaker was Mykhailo Cherniak, editor of the *Russkii holos* [Russian Voice] published in Edmonton. He spoke very insultingly about the Ukrainians, calling them blisters,

---

* The reference is to western Ukrainians who advocated the linguistic and cultural merger of Ukrainians with the Russians. (Ed.)

Mazepites* and greenhorns. After him spoke Fuyarchuk
[Fuiarchuk], a hotel owner from Edmonton, followed by the
Reverend Pantelei Bozhyk and Gospodin** Hladyk, who had come
from the United States to strengthen the spirit of "Russians" in
Alberta. The whole lot of them so slandered Ukrainians that even
though Ukrainian feeling in Alberta was then still largely dormant,
those present did not care for what was being said and protested.
When E. Kozlovsky, one of the Ukrainian teachers dismissed by
Fletcher, asked to speak, the chairman refused, although the
audience encouraged him to do so. And when Kozlovsky jumped on
the nearest farm wagon and began denouncing the previous
speakers, the "Russians" shouted, "Pull him off the wagon." At that
point, a relative of the MLA pulled Kozlovsky off and, in doing so,
broke Kozlovsky's glasses. To Kozlovsky's defence went Tanasko
Khamashchuk, a taxpayer for the Bukowina School, and a fight
broke out that ruined the celebration.

Bukowina School Trustees Go to Court in Edmonton

The Alberta government was convinced that all the trouble
among the 'meek' Ukrainians was caused by "Mazepites," because
this is what Ostrovsky had told the minister of education. So
Fletcher, as the official trustee, dragged the Bukowina School
trustees into court for paying their teacher sixty-five dollars after
they had been told they were no longer in charge of the school. The
trial was held in Edmonton before Judge Crawford, the
introductory part of whose judgment is reprinted here:

March 30, 1914

IN THE DISTRICT COURT OF THE
DISTRICT OF EDMONTON

FLETCHER
vs.
KUTCHER

JUDGMENT (ORAL)

This is a lawsuit arising out of a set of circumstances which seem to
be most unfortunate. The School District in question sought to have as

---

* Followers of Mazepa, a seventeenth-century Ukrainian ruler who tried
to free Ukraine from Russian domination through an alliance with
Sweden. (Ed.)
** Russian word for "Mister." (Ed.)

their teacher one of their own race and one of their own religion, and he could at the same time speak the English language so as to qualify in that respect as a teacher in one of our District Schools. For some reason or other, which I will not attempt even to guess, the Department of Education refused to grant him a permit. He was engaged, however, by the Board of the Local District by a resolution on their minute book and by a written contract entered into between him and the Board of Trustees, by the terms of which he was to be paid $65 per month. He taught during the months of May and June and until the 15th day of July under the terms of that contract. He was paid by the Trustees for the months of May and June and on the 11th day of July the Supervisor of Foreign Schools, as he is called, went out from the Department of Education and objected to the District having for their teacher Mr. Czumer, who was then in charge. Mr. Czumer, who is a man that impressed me very favorably, seems to be bright, intelligent and of an honest disposition; but the department, under the powers conferred upon it by the Act, interfered.

Now it is the duty of the Judge, not to make the law, but to interpret it, and, as far as in him lies, to administer it; and although it is not always administered according to its strictest letter, I understand his duty to be to construe it in the majority of cases according to its true spirit. The people of this Province have passed the Act, and the provisions of it are clear, and no judge can overrule those provisions. He must interpret them according to their plain ordinary meaning. A judge is only one man, and the Legislature is composed of many, and no judge has the right to set up his single and individual opinion against all the men composing a Legislature as to the advisability of the legislation that they have passed.

Women Take the Case of the Teacher into Their Own Hands

At the end of 1913, at a special session of the Legislature, Mr. Boyle had the School Act amended to ensure that all children of school age attended only those public and separate schools supervised by school inspectors appointed by the Department of Education. The private school at Bukowina became illegal and at Christmas its teacher Czumer said good-bye to the children and the community and moved to Edmonton.

At the same time Armstrong, the English teacher, went on holidays. He had remained at the school like someone under confinement, while being paid out of the district treasury by the official trustee. One evening, after he had returned from his vacation, a group of women who came to his place by the school pleaded with him to leave the district and not to cause any more trouble because they would not send their children to him.

Armstrong was an impudent and arrogant man. He told the women that it was not their business to give him orders, and he showed them the door. For this ungentlemanly behaviour, the women roughed him up a bit. He left the district that evening never to return.

Armstrong recognized one of the women—Mariia, the wife of Ivan Kapitsky, a native of Chornavka village, Chernivtsi County, Bukovyna—and laid a charge of "assault" against her. The trial was conducted in Vegreville by the same Judge Crawford, who sentenced her to two months in the women's prison at Macleod, Alberta. She served her time there with an eighteen-month-old child.

The *Edmonton Bulletin* wrote the following about this unpleasant affair:

DETERMINED TO HAVE RUTHENIAN TEACHERS ONLY

Women Maltreat English Teacher Who Had Taken Charge of School

REFUSED TO PAY TAXES FOR SCHOOL PURPOSES

Definite Outside Organization Determined to Break Up School System

During the year 1913 a large number of Russians and Ruthenians in the province of Manitoba, not qualified to teach school and most of them having a very imperfect knowledge of English, undertook to employ themselves in the various schools in the Ruthenian settlements of Alberta. They were promptly dismissed by Mr. Fletcher, superintendent of foreign schools, acting under instructions from the department of education. There can be little doubt now that there was a definite outside organization behind these people determined to break up the educational system of the province in so far as the Ruthenian districts were concerned. Bukowina school district appears to have been decided on for their purpose and in that case the teacher refused to quit. The school board made a disturbance and were fined in the courts but a qualified certificated teacher was installed in this school. The agitators there appear to have been supplied with money from some source because they erected a private school and installed an unqualified man to teach in it. The ratepayers refused to pay their taxes and the leaders among them threatened any that might pay and succeeded in intimidating the rest into refusal. Mr. Fletcher, who had been appointed official trustee after trying all peaceful means to collect the taxes, was obliged to resort to distress. This had the desired effect. A few horses were seized and after taking legal advice they paid up. The last move of the agitation was against the English teacher and women seem to have been employed as the instruments in this case. On January 4th when Mr. Armstrong returned to his shack alongside of the school house after the vacation, two women came into his shack and when his back was turned struck him on the head with a pot and proceeded to maul him up generally using their teeth upon him very fiercely. He succeeded in ejecting them from the house. He was then set upon by a couple of men with clubs who beat him up unmercifully. Of course, the offenders will be prosecuted.

These people are determined that nothing but Ruthenian schools shall be allowed to be conducted in that part of the country and are trying to make a test case out of Bukowina. The newspaper known as "Nowyny," a Russian publication in Edmonton, has been keeping the agitation warm for several months. This newspaper has been strongly advising against the use of English in the public schools and against qualified teachers, condemning the department of education for not establishing Ruthenian schools among these people.

The Ukrainians of Edmonton Protest

The persecution of Ukrainian school districts by J. R. Boyle was opposed not only by the taxpayers in the districts but by others. Only the Russophiles defended him.

The Ukrainians of Edmonton held a rally and drafted the following resolutions, which they forwarded to Mr. Stewart, the premier's deputy:

1. Not having anything against the teaching of the English language in the public schools in Ukrainian districts, we demand that besides the English language, the Ukrainian children be taught also their own language, and that for this there be employed teachers in the Ukrainian districts who are fluent in both English and Ukrainian.

2. We declare that the information given by the Alberta Department of Education to the English public through the English Liberal press, which gives the impression that Ukrainians are waging a battle against the English language, is absolutely false and calculated to arouse in English public opinion a feeling of hostility toward the Ukrainians so as to cover the uncivilized action of Minister Boyle with a halo of "patriotism."

3. We categorically protest the provocative action taken against Ukrainians in Alberta by Minister Boyle, who in his hatred of everything Ukrainian, stooped so low as to insult publicly all Ukrainians and their language by publishing at public expense a translation of the School Act in a language that not only the Ukrainians but no people in the world speak. It is the language of

traitors and renegades, used exclusively by provocateurs and paid agents of the Russian government to disseminate the glorification of the tsar among Ukrainians and to support the lie that there is no such thing as a Ukrainian nation, but only "Little Russians" who speak a Russian dialect.

4. We declare that we will not tolerate further provocation from the Department of Education until we are shown respect for our language and our civil liberties.

Chairman: N. Andriiv
Secretary: H. Michalyshyn [Mykhailyshyn]

A Poem Written During the Persecution of Ukrainian Teachers in Alberta in 1914

"English Culture"

There are those in Alberta
Who want
To extinguish our Ukrainian spirit.
They are always thinking
Of how to destroy the Ukrainian language
And all that is sacred to us.
Dismissing Ukrainian teachers from their schools
Is their main business.

Do not do this to us.
We are not cattle!
Will learning English alone
Make a child wise?
Propagandists of culture and pedagogy,
Do you not know that
We are people of a different character
With our own Ukrainian sensibility,
Our own way of thinking,
And a culture different from yours.
You have got assimilation in mind,
But these are not the old days.
You could get away with this in the Middle Ages
With others, not with us.
We are not Irish or Scots,
We are sons of sacred Rus'.

You killed the language
Of those people,
But you did not make them English.
We are not like them,

We are not of the kind you can kill.
Neither now nor ever will you destroy us.
As long as the sun shines in the sky,
As long as you and we shall live.

Why can the French and Germans
Learn their own language in Canada?
Remember this, Englishmen,
That what is ours belongs to us.

We helped Canada rise
In commerce and all things;
We are not going to offer ourselves
As sacrificial lambs.
We will learn our own.
We are not going to become laughingstocks
By giving ourselves up to you as a sacrifice
To shame our people, to sin before God.

The world will know you
For what you really are.
We will tell the whole world:
"English culture is peculiar."

"Kruk,"Vegreville, Alberta
Novyny, 21 March 1914

From the Edmonton *Capital*, 9 April 1914:

COMPLETE ENDORSATION OF THE MINISTER OF EDUCATION

Meeting Attended by Over 500 Russians, Little Russians and Poles,
Approves Action Taken by Department of Education Relating to
Education of Children of Foreign-Born Parents

At a meeting attended by over five hundred Russians, Little Russians, and Poles, held at Rabbit Hill on Tuesday last, a resolution was passed strongly approving not only the stand the Hon. J. R, Boyle, minister of education, has taken with regard to education matters, but also commending the general policy of the provincial government. The meeting was of a most representative character, those in attendance coming from Rabbit Hill, Bufford, Leduc, Glidehurst and other places in the neighborhood. The following resolution was passed:

"Resolved, that this meeting of Russians, Little Russians, and Poles fully endorses the policy of the present provincial government of Alberta.

"Holding in esteem the laws of our great country, of which we are citizens, we want to understand those laws, and therefore we return many thanks to the government of Alberta, which does not spare energy and expense in printing the ordinances in our native language. Specially we return many thanks to the Hon. J. R. Boyle, minister of education, that he in such weighty affairs as the school ordinance, considered the feelings of our people and printed the same in the etymological system of spelling, which we all understand, and which we all learned in the public schools in Austria.

"We assure the Hon. J. R. Boyle and his government of our affections, and when the proper time comes we will revenge ourselves upon the enemy, and will repay with gratitude to the Hon. J. R. Boyle and his government the respect of the sentiments of our people.

"We further express with clearness the contempt we have of all ungraduated Austrian nurslings like Messrs. Kramar [*sic*], Svarich, Rudyk, Krakiwski [*sic*], Stechishin, etc., who, to the advantage of Austria in the old country, learned to betray their own people, and who here, in Canada, through their Conservative newspaper, "Nowyny," want to divide us into parts."

> (Signed)JOHN WORKUN, Chairman
> JOHN PYRCH, Secretary*

Ukrainian Children Driven Out of School

The year 1913 was a memorable one for Ukrainians in Alberta. They elected their first MLA and had their teachers and children driven out of school. The *Vegreville Observer* of 10 [15] October 1913 contained the following "resolution" of the Vegreville School Board:

> The report pointed out that out of an enrolment of 251 at the school, there was a non-resident attendance of 76 or substantially 30% of the whole. In the lower standards alone, the enrolment of non-resident pupils was 25% of the whole .... In addition to this it was shown in the report that 80% of the non-resident pupils are of foreign extraction.

---

* Czumer's account, though shorter and phrased ,differently, is equally partisan in tone and is retained because the meaning is essentially the same. In the *Capital*, neither Workun nor Pyrch is mentioned and the headline reads as follows: "FEW RUTHENIANS ARE OPPOSED TO BOYLE'S POLICY/Much Barking by Conservative Newspaper, But Bite Not Feared/Russians of All Creeds Pass Strong Resolution/Attempt of Disgruntled ones to Discredit Department over Translation." (Ed.)

Whatever the merits of these pupils may be, their attendance at the school is clearly detrimental to the progress of those pupils who belong to the district. Their imperfect knowledge of English makes it necessary for the teachers to expend much time with them .... In other respects also the presence of such a large number of children of foreign extraction is not in the best interest of the schools .... That owing to the congested condition of the school and for the other reasons mentioned in the report, notice be sent to those interested, that after the close of the present school term all non-resident pupils of foreign extraction will be excluded from the school, and that the attendance of non-resident English speaking pupils be a matter of further investigation.

High odours due to the liking of some of the pupils for those vegetables which may be accounted as smelly, have been a source of annoyance to some of the teachers. The board empowers the teachers to chase the offenders from the school until such time as this olfractory offence is rectified.

And that is how the situation in Alberta's schools once looked with respect to Ukrainian pioneer "interlopers."

~ 10 ~

What the English Missionaries Once Wrote

The English Methodist magazine for young people, *Onward,* published in Toronto, contained an article in November 1913 ["The Ruthenians in Alberta"] that was translated into Ukrainian in *Novyny* of 1 November 1913:

On approaching one of the dwellings one is in dire danger of being torn to pieces by a pack of wolfish, hungry-looking dogs. Should he escape these and open the door, several chickens start out noisily under his feet, and he beholds an old hen and her brood resting under the stove. In another corner a turkey is mothering her brood, and a family of kittens are playing on the earthen floor. A youngster or two are perched on the bed; three or four unkempt, dirty urchins cling to their mother's skirts and gaze curiously at the newcomer. The whole establishment reeks with a strong, peculiar Russian odor. If it is about their meal time, the home-made table is freighted with an unlimited supply of boiled eggs, some brown rye or barley bread and a copious supply of musky tea. The most noticeable feature of the dwelling and its occupants is the lack of cleanliness everywhere in evidence.

Though hospitable to a stranger, in their dealings with each other they often display the most remarkable avarice, which would shame even a Jew. Dr. Archer, of Lamont, the nearest town to the district, told us of an incident which well illustrates this. On one occasion a Ruthenian's wife lay very sick. Not wishing to leave her alone while he took the trail to the doctor's, the man requested his neighbor's wife to stay with her. This neighbor, however, forced him to first pay her an adequate sum for the valuable time she was losing, before consenting. It is said that they even levy toll for giving a neighbor a ride, but the writer cannot vouch for the truth of this statement. Business men attest that they are fairly honest, but all alike agree that if a "Russian" does not pay cash, but informs you that he will pay on a certain day, he has no intention of ever keeping his promise.[...]

Three of us were distinguished guests at one of their weddings.[...] We were invited to share in the wedding feast, and sat down to a table on which were placed several dishes of unsavory-looking meat, some bridal bread (their wedding cake), which resembled doughnuts, and glasses of foaming beer, which we found some difficulty in refusing, as all Galicians drink large quantities, especially on such occasions. A dish of garlic, called "saeur-kraut" [*sic*], was also in evidence, which proved fairly eatable, though its appearance reminded one rather painfully of what the hogs dine on in Ontario.[...]

Obviously the task of Canadianizing this Slavic people, of giving them Canadian ideals and mode of living, is largely the work of the school teacher.[...] Here is an opportunity for Canada's young student manhood to show their patriotism and obtain a summer's experience worth while by spending their vacations in aiding in the naturalization of these thirty thousand foreigners.[...]

How This Patriotism Was Shown

The Ukrainian newspaper *Novyny* carried the following news item on 29 August 1913:

The Cruel Crime of a "Qualified" Teacher

Last Monday, 25 August, at noon, W. H., his wife and nine-year-old daughter came to Peter Svarich's office in Vegreville, Alberta, and told him the unbelievable story of what had happened earlier that morning in the Kolomea School from which Fletcher had recently dismissed a Ukrainian teacher, replacing him with an agent, who not long ago was selling patent medicine of his own make in Montreal. The teacher, instead of teaching, was corrupting the children.

After hearing the story, Mr. Svarich immediately went to the local magistrate, presented the information, secured a warrant for the teacher's arrest and, going immediately by car with a police officer to the Kolomea School, arrested the renegade teacher, W. Dukenman, at three o'clock in the afternoon.

After a preliminary hearing the judge decided to send the accused to the Fort* and to refer the case to a higher court for trial by jury.

---

* The gaol at Fort Saskatchewan. (Ed.)

The *Novyny* editor's own comment follows: "This is a brief but striking example of the qualified English teacher whom Mr. Boyle praises to the heavens and thrusts violently amongst Ruthenians in order to civilize them. A fine civilization. If a Negro in the States had acted in the same way, then the civilized White English would have lynched him at once . . . . "

Miscellaneous

The glorious past of some nations eventually turns out not to be as glorious as once described. There are people who are capable of falsifying and whitewashing the history of their ancestors in the same way as they "improve" butter by adding artificial colouring.

In these recollections of our settlers in Western Canada, which show both the good and the bad, we find nothing that would shame Ukrainians or place them lower than others. And when others tried to show us in a bad light, it was only to whitewash themselves.

The Ukrainian pioneers are leaving the history of their first half-century in Canada unfalsified because the things they can boast about today and of which their descendants can be proud, they got by hard, honest labour.

Professor Petro Karmansky of Galicia, who lived in Canada but could not get used to Canadian life, wrote a lot about the behaviour and experiences of both Ukrainians and Canadians which he described in a series of articles entitled, "The Monkey's Mirror." When he finally got fed up with life in Canada, he left. At the end of his stay he wrote the following poem:

Farewell Canada

Canada, land of falsehood and stupidity,
The market place of ideals, conscience and honour;
Where one must sacrifice to a frenzied mob
All that is holy and without regret
And come to love this enemy and this foreign land.

Canada, sly and vile coquette,
Having lured with lewd cries
Unlucky victims to your mud,
Slash their hearts with deep cutting lashes
Of insults, slander, scorn and baseness
From the mouths of ignorant rabble.

I love you! I love you for the sufferings of the people
Who tilled your prairie with their blood,
For all the villainy, betrayal and deception
Of your sons, who in cold blood
Deal in human beings, like dumb cattle,
And prosper from human sweat and death.

I love you for the yearning that burns in exiles,
For their days of silent sorrow and despair
In the face of lies and shameless robbery,
For their struggle with ignorant and wild masses,
And for their triumph over darkness and falsehood.

I love you and bless you, Canada,
And leave your shores in sadness.
Here my strength was fortified in the battle
Which I willingly and gladly raised.
In it I have seen the sure path to my salvation,
And the promises of your resurrection.

Farewell Canada! It is hard to leave
With a broken heart your fate's grave
In which are laid to rest my silent pains.
To curse you for all my painful losses,
To curse the crowd that sucked the joy from my heart
Is pointless: It knows not what it does.

Novyny, 12 May 1914

Get The Facts Before Signing
(News Item from the *Edmonton Journal,* 1941)

The School Board of Hampton district, five miles north of Bowmanville, Ontario, engaged Miss Mariika Kozak, a talented, nineteen-year-old teacher from Oshawa, to teach in their school. But before anyone knew a thing about it, someone took it upon himself to go among the taxpayers and collect signatures opposed to Miss Kozak's appointment, because she had a foreign name and her parents were of foreign ancestry. Ninety out of a hundred taxpayers signed a petition to the trustees asking that Miss Kozak be kept out of the school. Since she had already signed a contract with the trustees, she asked for the indemnity due her according to the contract. Although the school board had to pay her 180 dollars, the English "patriots" stood by their decision not to accept Miss Kozak into their school.

Miss M. Kozak was of Ukrainian ancestry, though not a Catholic, as alleged. She was a Protestant, a member of the United Church, with a brother in the Canadian army. None of this convinced the chauvinist mind of British "fair play," which refused to accept her.

There was a great deal of publicity about this in such Anglo-Ontario newspapers as the *Ottawa Journal*, the *Toronto Star*, the *Woodstock Sentinel Review*, the *Hamilton Spectator*, the *London Free Press*, the *Peterborough Examiner* and others, and all of them disapproved of the action taken by the Hamptonians. Nevertheless, for Canadians of Ukrainian descent the fact remains that it will take another half century before British chauvinism in Canada disappears from some foolish minds. What George Bernard Shaw wrote in *The Man of Destiny* is true:

> He [the Englishman] is never at a loss for an effective moral attitude .... There is nothing so bad or so good that you will not find Englishmen doing it; but you will never find an Englishman in the wrong. He does everything on principle. He fights on patriotic principles; he robs you on business principles; he enslaves you on imperial principles; ...

~11~

The Political Process in the Whitford District of Alberta

During the provincial election of 1913 in Alberta, Paul Rudyk, who ran as an Independent Liberal candidate in Whitford, was "arrested" on a charge of fraud brought by someone named Gordichuk [Gordeichuk] concerning a money order at the Edmonton post office.

Paul Rudyk was known by every Ukrainian colonist in Alberta. Whenever a Ukrainian got into trouble he would turn to Rudyk for help. Because Edmonton was centrally located, it was the place of all business transactions. Paul Rudyk lived there and helped workers and farmers willingly and without charge, cashing cheques and sending money orders to the Old Country.

It so happened that a money order for forty dollars belonging to Gordichuk was returned from Ottawa to Edmonton. The post office searched for the sender and found another Gordichuk, who also came from Bukovyna and had a wife there named Mariia. Although he assumed that this was probably not his money, for he had once sent his wife eighty dollars, he decided that since it was money he might as well keep it. Since he did not have a receipt, he asked Paul Rudyk to endorse the money order as his witness. The unsuspecting Rudyk signed it and the man cashed it. Rudyk did not know him personally and had never seen him before. Hundreds of people came to him with similar problems.

During the election of 1913, when the rightful owner of the

money returned from his job to Edmonton and learned at the post office that his money order had been returned from Ottawa and cashed by Rudyk, he demanded that Rudyk return his money. This surprised Rudyk, for he had forgotten all about it. He could not, however, deny it because the fellow had his receipt. It took a week for him to find the other Gordichuk. The mail carrier, Iliia Bodnaruk, who knew almost every resident on his route, helped Rudyk find the unlawful "owner" of the money order, who without arguing returned the money to the rightful owner.

During the heated political campaign, Rudyk's opponents used the incident to their advantage. On the telephone, they blew it out of all proportions, telling the people throughout the riding not to vote for Paul Rudyk because he could not be elected since he was under arrest. This undoubtedly was why Rudyk lost the election. The "arrest" took place the day before the election.

After the election Paul Rudyk asked the court to void the election. The hearing dragged on for several months and finally Judge Hyman ruled that during the election the elected MLA, Andrew Shandro, in the person of his agents, had spread false rumours about Rudyk, and new elections would therefore have to be held. A. Shandro had to pay the court costs.

Paul Rudyk decided not to run in the bye-election because of the objections of his ailing wife. Roman Kremar, editor of *Novyny*, ran in his place as a Conservative candidate against Andrew Shandro, who was re-elected (Kremar 472, Shandro 686). He represented the Whitford district until 1921, when he was defeated by Wasyl [Vasyl] Chornohuz, a farmer from Desjarlais, who was a candidate for the United Farmers of Alberta.

The Aftermath of Russophile Politics in Alberta: An Open Letter to Gospodin Hladyk

My Former Friend and Father of Katsaps!*

I received your letter with your declarations, exhortations and orders, and in the *Russkii narod* [Russian People] I read your revelations, rebukes and admonitions, but none of them hurt or frightened me because I knew well in advance that, after leaving your party, I would

---

* A derogatory term used by Ukrainians to describe Russians in general and particularly members of the Russian Orthodox church in Canada. (Ed.)

be exposed to many slanderous attacks from you and the rest of the katsaps.

To be honest, your cries have neither meaning nor value among the Ukrainian Orthodox people, because since my declaration I have received tens of letters from real Orthodox people, natives of Bukovyna, expressing congratulations and supporting my resignation, but to make the matter clear to you and to justify my behaviour, I declare once more that I have not abandoned my people, nor my people's history, nor the Orthodox faith of my forefathers but have only disowned the katsaps and their dirty work. This is clear enough for even a small child to understand. I have returned to my former position for which all of Alberta knew me prior to 1913, when you came to Alberta. Up to that time all we Orthodox, both from Bukovyna and Galicia, together with our reverend fathers, considered ourselves Ruthenian-Ukrainians of the Greek Orthodox faith and no one had ever heard of the katsapism of Moscophiles until you spread it across Canada, starting to my misfortune right in my own locality. Until your appearance, I was a supporter of the Ukrainian movement as witnessed by my subscription to Ukrainian newspapers and my being a shareholder in the *Ukrainskyi holos*, my donation at the community hall in Vegreville to the "Ukrainian School" [in Lviv] and my purchase of a number of square metres of land for the Ukrainian Garden in Galicia. I did not have the slightest inkling of katsapism until you confused me and led me off the right track.

As long as I was Ukrainian, I was respected and honoured among the people and had many friends. My business flourished and I prospered and God blessed me in my family life. But since the devil brought Cherniak and you to these parts, and since you succeeded in twisting the minds of our reverend fathers and their parishioners, swaying me and a few others to your side and using us for your dirty, rotten work, then everything has gone wrong for me, and I have profited on your politics as much as Zablotsky profited on selling soap.* Because of your katsap politics, I have lost my old friends, some having become my bitter enemies. For instance, I believe that Mr. Rudyk would not have gone into such a long and costly court action against me if it had not been for you. Nor would William Czumer have annoyed me and gotten under my skin, and I would not have had to take revenge on him if it had not been for you. Stechishin and Kremar would not have compared me to dirt nor would the *Ukrainskyi holos* have sharpened its daggers at my expense had it not been for your politics; nor would there have been so much grief and animosity in my family, so much discord between the people and the clergy in the Orthodox congregations and so much argument and hatred among our people had it not been for your

---

* A proverb indicating he had suffered considerable loss. (Ed.)

devilish politics. Finally, I have to add—because I am speaking as sincerely as at confession—that from the time of my involvement with you, I have felt the wrath of God in my private life. My wife, who before this was a workhorse of a woman who took care of the entire farm, suddenly became ill and after long years of serious sickness, expensive operations and cures, died, leaving me with six small children. Because of the court proceedings, I lost a considerable amount of property. Luck willed that my house burn down and through neglect I lost a considerable number of cattle and horses. There were times when my own life was endangered: once a gasoline engine exploded and at another time a gasoline drum blew high in the air and dropped only inches from my nose. These could be called accidents, but so many of them happened to me in a short time that people have attached a lot of significance to them and have considered them God's punishment for my sins. I am an ordinary man, so my sins are no greater than that of others, but since I have had more than my share of punishment, this must be a result of having disowned my name, family, history, people and of having become a katsap renegade.

I have especially felt in my heart the wrong that you and the rest of your katsap gang have done and continue to do to sincere Ukrainians by slandering them without cause before the government, calling them traitors, enemies of Great Britain, Austrians and supporters of the Germans. You accuse them of being Mazepites and bumpkins and insult them with derogatory names. Besides, how much venom and ill will do you pour on the Uniates [Greek Catholics] and their bishops, who do not deserve any of it and have every human and God-given right to be what they are.

All this came to weigh so heavily upon my soul that I decided to do what I did. I abandoned katsapism, not for insignificant or light reasons or for political considerations to ensure victory on the eve of the elections. I did it out of sincere good will and for the national good, for the good of the enslaved and dismembered Mother Ukraine.

A. S. Shandro.
MLA and Lieutenant of the 218th Batallion
Ukrainskyi holos, 7 February 1917

Ukraine's Sorrow

Even though I make light of my misfortune,
It keeps growing;
My children are gone all over the world,
Oh, what are they doing there?

Some have sold themselves to the Poles
And shun me.
Others serve Moscow loyally,
Digging my grave.

The Turk ruined me; the Pole finished me off
And the Moscovite lured me
By faith in the Tsar,
And then betrayed me.

And in Canada
The Moscovite, Pole, Englishman, Frenchman
And various bandits
Take care of my children,
Not allowing them to live.

When will there be justice,
The bandura play,
Fate and freedom smile,
And truth shine?

Pavlo Melnyk
Myrnam, Alberta
Novyny, 1 July 1913

~12~

The Debate Over Assimilating Ukrainians

The following appeared in the *Western Home Monthly* of October 1913:

> The parents and the state are jointly responsible for the education of the child and if the educational machinery be insufficient it must be supplemented with efficient machinery.[...]Since the English language is the speech of Western Canada, it should be obligatory upon the state to insist upon every foreign child acquiring such a knowledge of English as will give him an "equality of opportunity" with the English-speaking child. The greatest factor in the assimilation of the foreign born child is a knowledge of an ability to use, in every affair of life—the English speech. Assimilation begins with the public school where the English tongue is the sole instrument of instruction.[...]The conditions prevailing in Western Canada, in these foreign areas, are a disgrace and constitute a serious menace to the West's future welfare.[...]Canadian ideals and standards of national life are threatened with extinction. They, the progeny of the foreign born people, increase and multiply like the Israelites in Egypt, with astonishing rapidity. The foreign born already control electoral divisions and they are beginning to dare the right of Canadians to assail the entrenched position of prejudice and ignorance.[...]Is the Canadian going to be held in thrall by a foreign incomer at the command of a church which is a strange mixture of religion, commercialism and lust for civil power?

Whom the *Western Home Monthly* considered Canadians and whom foreign intruders, it is not difficult to guess, though no explanation was provided. As for the true "Canadians," it would have to be the Indians, whom the Europeans found here four hundred years before the arrival of such as the Ukrainians.

At the same time that the *Western Home Monthly* was concerned about foreigners in Western Canada, an article by E. W. Thomson appeared in the *Boston Transcript* [see *Vegreville Observer*, 15 October 1913] in defence of Ukrainian teachers in Alberta:

> Boyle attacked their schools, which were being expertly conducted by bilingual teachers, who had spent three years studying in English normal schools and undoubtedly could teach the English language to Ukrainian children faster than unilingual English teachers. It is known throughout the West that Ukrainians are very anxious for their children to learn English.[...]They themselves brought in and want to continue employing bilingual Ukrainian teachers in their schools. [These teachers, if they had not been persecuted, would naturally have wanted to teach the children English as quickly as possible.]*
>
> In the West I had an opportunity to talk with a large number of Ukrainians of all ages and walks of life. There is no people in that boundless space that is more pleasant or whose children are raised with such attractive characteristics.

An Address About Ukrainians by Mr. Coldwell, Minister of Education in Manitoba, to the Anglican Church Synod in Winnipeg, 1913**

> I take the liberty of appealing to the synod that we conduct ourselves according to the British principle of respecting as much as possible the aspirations and feelings of these people and treating them with the same understanding we would wish for ourselves if we were in their country.
>
> You cannot drive these people any more than you can drive the British people. First you have to gain their trust and then you can do them the good you want.
>
> There was a method used here called "Kick-these-people-around,"

---

* Part of the original omitted by Czumer. (Ed.)
** The source is not given and efforts to trace it have been unsuccessful. There is no evidence that Mr. Coldwell addressed the Anglican synod in 1913. (Ed.)

but this is the last thing that should be done if you want them to become good British subjects. If you get closer to them, as you should, they will come to value British ways and customs and will be convinced that they are good for them.

I protest against forced assimilation. On the contrary, we should proceed according to British tradition and allow them as much freedom as possible, so that they retain at least the moral law.

One Ukrainian's View of Assimilation Published in the Ukrainian Press of the Time

There is a lot of talk today about nationalism, about schools, about safeguarding the Ukrainian people from assimilation. Those who do not want to believe in our separateness here on this side of the ocean are not completely mistaken either.

There is no doubt that the upbringing of coming generations in which we place our hopes for the future should be in harmony with the natural needs and aspirations of the people.

So that our descendants would not be weakened or spiritually crippled, our teachers must be properly prepared, of strong character and independent, not slaves, footstools and party hacks. Whatever they instil in the tender soul of a child will develop into the deepest roots. The teacher is the sun's rays on sprouting seeds. Teachers play a vital role in national education and revival. They give direction to the future life of a child, who must grow up to become a true citizen, an honest member of his national family.

The teacher should awaken in the child a feeling of beauty, of love in his heart, and throw out the embryo of all fanaticism. The child should be raised in such a way that he or she will understand the evil of coercion and egoism, whether religious, political or class.

The education of our children in Canada to be loyal citizens and true patriots has to lie in the good education and ability of teachers. To achieve this, the teachers must be independent, strong-willed and possess a deep sense of self-reliance, respect for self and others. We parents must take special care that our children do not come out of our schools morally crippled or with their nationality warped. How long we will retain our national identity in Canada will depend on the type of child that comes out of our schools.

How we conduct our affairs will be clear proof of our power in developing future generations of those who carry a Ukrainian name. Neither party strife nor sectarian hatred will keep us alive. The basis for true progress is the good and wise education of children.

D. Ia.

The assimilation of Ukrainians in Canada was mainly the concern of the Protestant churches. From the above examples we can see how the Ukrainian pioneer in Canada had to suffer a great deal listening to and reading all kinds of slander directed against him. We record this in these recollections not only as "exhibits," but so that our grandchildren will know what happened during the first twenty-five years of Ukrainian life in Western Canada.

The Ukrainian Orthodox Church Appears in Canada

In talking about the past experiences of Ukrainian settlers in Canada, it is time to mention one important aspect of our social life—the church—which after so many internal problems and struggles against foreign influence came to the forefront and played a leading role in religious patriotism.

From the beginning of Ukrainian immigration to Canada, the religious battle has been almost continuous, always changing. Ukrainians came to Canada as Ruthenian-Galician Greek Catholics or Ruthenian-Bukovynian Orthodox, but in the first fifty years they either changed to or renamed themselves Ukrainian Catholics or Ukrainian Orthodox or Russian Orthodox. There were also Ukrainian Protestants, Pentecostals, Seventh Day Adventists and God-knows-what-else.

For other people, especially the English, this religious division did not have much influence on national [i.e., group] unity because their goals were different. Such changes affected Ukrainians more deeply because the divisions had not developed from within but from without, and they infiltrated the people to destroy their solidarity. It has always been a trauma, but instead of trying to rid ourselves of this foreign influence, the Ukrainians in Canada have fought relentlessly among themselves to the astonishment of others. In this battle, national "patriotism" has always played an important role.

From the beginning, the Ukrainian missionary Basilian fathers tried to eradicate Russian Orthodox and Protestant influence among the Ukrainian Greek Catholics in Canada and relentlessly denounced all who agreed with the foreign influence. If our Ukrainian Greek Catholic church had been truly independent of a foreign hierarchy at the time, it would undoubtedly have overcome all the problems from the start, and who knows if it would not have united all the Orthodox Ukrainians from Bukovyna. Unfortunately, this did not happen and perhaps because of this there will always be an interminable religious battle until people learn that nationality is one thing and religion or church another.

To rid itself more easily of foreign influence and avoid total national disintegration, Ukrainian "patriotism" decided that its own independent church was the only salvation of Ukrainians in Canada. Such a church had been considered before there were any Greek Catholic or Orthodox priests in Canada. The idea went through all kinds of trials, but it was difficult to realize until the fall of the tsarist regime in Russia in 1917.

With the loss of its Russian head, the Russian Orthodox mission in Canada began to weaken and lose ground, because its flow of financial support had dried up. It was then that the more nationally conscious Ukrainians conceived and organized the "Ukrainian Orthodox Brotherhood" to propagate the idea of establishing in Canada a national "Ukrainian Autocephalous Orthodox Church" among the Orthodox and disgruntled Ukrainian leaders in other churches. Patterned after the church that once existed in Ukraine and which, after the revolution of 1917, began to exist in the Soviet Union, the idea for a similar church in Canada was born, it is said, in St. Julien, Saskatchewan, with its sponsors being P. Shvydky and Wasyl Swystun, the rector of the Petro Mohyla Ukrainian Institute in Saskatoon. At a meeting of the Institute in 1918, the subject was fully debated. Four "Russian" priests [Ukrainian priests in the Russian Orthodox church] were present and all but Reverend Kiziun supported the idea.

The Ukrainian Orthodox Brotherhood conducted its work so successfully that in 1918 the Reverend Ivan German, originally from Bukovyna, converted three congregations in Alberta—Suchava, Shepyntsi [Shepenge] and Kolomea—to become the first congregations of the Ukrainian Orthodox church in Canada.

~13~

The Role of Ukrainian Pioneers as Farmers in Canada

The role played by Ukrainian settlers in Canada merits careful attention because they came, as they themselves said, with only the ten fingers on their hands and nothing else. Yet in their fifty years in this country they made great strides forward, not easily but through suffering and hard work. Their role at the time was that of hard labourers—cultivators of the western reaches of the wilderness, which they turned into fertile fields of wheat.

The central Europeans were brought to Western Canada when it was clear that other colonists could not conquer the "Great West." They were brought like those volunteer "storm troopers" who, as the last resort, break through a strongly fortified battle line in war to capture enemy terrain. They were brought like African slaves of the seventeenth and eighteenth centuries had been brought to the southern United States to create vast plantations of cotton, tobacco and corn. The Ukrainian colonists played a similar role in the forests and wide open prairies of Western Canada. They were called by various names: "Galicians," "Ruthenians," "Bukovynians," "Russians" and "Central Europeans," but their role was the same—to conquer or perish. And they conquered, throwing themselves at the Canadian West like daredevils, transforming its vast wilderness into fertile fields sown with golden kernels of wheat and other grains. Today Western Canada is the granary for Western Europe.

And did anybody then worry about these "Galicians"? No. They broke the land with their own strength, without help from the government, by the sweat of their brow, in cold and hunger, thereby attracting the attention of the civilized world. The following few lines bear witness to their great struggle. They were written by an English teacher, who taught in those early years in an area settled by Ukrainians. Among other things, she said, "Galician children came to school in dirty patched-over rags, buttoned with nails, and in worn-out footwear held together with binder twine. They were sickly and old in appearance, with faces worn with work and without the least interest in children's games."

The extreme poverty this teacher described among the Ukrainian pioneers in Western Canada proves that few at the time cared about what happened to the colonists. Seventy-five years before Ukrainian immigration to Western Canada, they cared differently about non-"Galician" immigrants to Eastern Canada. Here is what W. G. Smith wrote in his book *A Study in Canadian Immigration*, published in 1920, about the Scottish colony of Lanark on the Clyde:

> Lanark on the Clyde was a colony composed exclusively of Scottish families who settled in 1821 near Lake Huron in Ontario. The population of the colony was 166 men, 134 women and 532 children.
>
> To maintain the colony, in the first year the British government sent them provisions for a whole year, forty dollars per adult and all the implements necessary for farming such as ploughs, harrows, wagons and sleighs. As well they supplied 40 hand-turned millstones for grinding grain into flour; 40 cross-cut saws for sawing trees; 12 rip-saws for cutting logs into boards; 157 axes, gimlets and broad axes, both large and small; hammers, picks, hoes, spades, rakes and other necessities.*

The government considered them "undesirable," so it showed no concern. They came as cannon fodder for steamship agents, railroad companies and land speculators.

Although others also came to the "free" lands of Western Canada—particularly from Eastern Canada, the United States and Western Europe—they came well-organized with capital and all the

---

* Despite extensive research, the source of this quotation is not known. It is not in W. G. Smith, *A Study in Canadian Immigration* (Toronto: Ryerson Press, 1920). (Ed.)

things needed to establish farms quickly. The average Ukrainian settler found himself in a different situation. When we read in English newspapers and magazines and other publications of the time about "poor Galicians," the pitiful state in which our poor colonists found themselves in Western Canada is confirmed. How else could it have been?

To find oneself far across the sea in an unknown, foreign land of wilderness and forest, without adequate security for sustaining oneself and one's large family of little children, was a daring act on the part of the first "Galicians," a risk that would have strained anyone's nerves, for considering their circumstances it did appear that they would not survive. Some Canadians watched skeptically as if it was none of their concern; others seeing the deplorable conditions of the poverty-stricken colonies complained to the government, which had as much effect as whipping water. The general attitude was that these people should be left to their own devices. If they survived, then "all right"; and if they did not, it was no great loss.

But a great miracle happened! The "Galician" survived, though under the new name "Ukrainian." For his heroic accomplishments he received great acclaim, not only in print from interested journalists but even from the Canadian government. While these recollections were being written, the prime minister of Canada, W. L. Mackenzie King, in one of his "Canada at War" speeches, said that Western Canada, in proportion to its population, distinguished itself by sending more sons to war and supplying more bread, meat and foodstuffs for the Allied armies in Europe while also not lagging behind Eastern Canada in the war effort.

About the same time that Prime Minister King was praising the West, H. E. Spencer of Edgerton, Alberta, was speaking on the same matter to the School Trustees' Association of Alberta in Edmonton (11 November 1942). Comparing the profits of western farming with other industries in Canada, he showed statistically that the farmer in the West was wronged and exploited at the same time that other producers, especially eastern manufacturers, enjoyed substantial profits. His figures showed that from 1926 to 1929 the average farmer had an annual income of $791. From 1930 to 1940 it was only $329. In 1913 a binder cost $167 in Alberta and to buy it a farmer had to sell 261 bushels of wheat. In 1940 it was necessary to sell 637 bushels of wheat to buy a binder costing $340. In

1919 a farmer received a third of his gross income, in 1929 only a sixth and in 1940 barely a tenth, while manufacturers enjoyed nine-tenths of their gross.

Looking at the above figures carefully, we come to the conclusion that just as the worker and farmer were exploited during the pioneer period, so today the East has no mercy on the West.

Agriculture: The Mother of Culture

Without a doubt, agriculture, as history has shown, is the foundation of civilization. Before human culture can exist there must be agriculture. Since man relies on nature for survival, he is forced to act in favour of life. Wherever there is extensive, developed agriculture, the state and the nation are always secure.

Even the Bible notes that, as long as agriculture in the Euphrates valley was wisely managed, it fed half the world of the time. As soon as agriculture declined, civilization declined, including Canaan, the promised land of milk and honey, to which Moses led the Jews for forty years.

Because they had always engaged in agriculture, the Ukrainian people survived for centuries, standing up to the invasion of the Asiatic hordes and thereby defending also Western Europe. Wherever fate deposited a Ukrainian, beside his cottage there immediately appeared a vegetable garden with potatoes, buckwheat, cabbage and millet, and fields sown with rye, barley and wheat.

The Ukrainians who emigrated to Western Canada at the end of the nineteenth century based their society on agriculture. Right from the start they planted vegetable gardens, which was not the case among other immigrants of the time. The task of the Ukrainian settler was to develop agriculture in the boundless wilderness of the Far West. Why else were they brought there!

Contemporary wars have been fought between the great powers exclusively for control of industrious, agricultural nations. Without agriculture there would be no industrial progress.

In our own country, in various government reports and announcements one always notices the question, "How's the crop this year?" If the crop means so much that it worries manufacturers, grain speculators, railway directors and inspectors, steamship companies and even the government itself, then the status of the agricultural producer must be high. That agriculture has been considered the lowest occupation till now may be the result of everyone trying to take advantage of the farmer, as Mr. Spencer noted in his speech.

Here is what one Ukrainian pioneer in Western Canada wrote about the lot of the farmer:

The Farmer's Lot

Oh land of ours,
You field stacks of wheat.
You are rich,
Yet, why are we poor?

Oh land, we cut you
Eternally with the plough,
And you are always rich.
But what of that do we get?

For our toil you tell us
To feed everyone with your yields.
But why do we plod behind the plough
Hungry?

Where Did the First Kernel of Wheat Come From?

Since agriculture is the mother of all culture and since Ukrainians have been bound to this industry from time immemorial and will remain tied to it for the forseeable future, it is of interest to know the origins of wheat and who brought it to North America, and particularly Canada.

Professor N. I. Vavylov, a Russian research scientist who studied the origins of the wheat kernel, says that wheat originated in the Himalayan Mountains of Asia, the Abyssinian Mountains of Eastern Africa and in the mountains of Central and South America.

Other scholars claim that the ancient Greeks and Romans also engaged in cultivating wheat. When their culture began to decline, the cultivation of wheat was undertaken by the nations of Asia Minor bordering on the Black Sea and Southern Europe, which included the Ukrainians.

With the development of agriculture, nations flourished. During the reign of the Ukrainian princes, there was prosperity and people lived well. Their neighbours became envious and set out to destroy Ukrainian culture and rule the country.

A variety of European wheat was brought to North America in 1605 by the first French colonists who settled in Nova Scotia. It took a lot of care to acclimatize European wheat. It was not until 1842 that David Fife of Peterborough, Ontario, obtained some seed from Northern Europe and grew it here. It later found its way to Western Canada via Minnesota. Today that wheat is called Red Fife and matures in 120 days. Later, scientists crossed Red Fife with Red Calcutta to develop Marquis wheat, which ripened in 107 days. Nowadays there are several other varieties of wheat in Canada—Red Bob which matures in 101 days, Reward in 99 days and Garnett in 97 days.

The first Ukrainian colonists to raise wheat in Canada lived in the district of Beaver Creek at the Edna Post Office, now Star, Alberta. Dr. J. Oleskiw mentions this in his book *O emigratsii*, which he wrote in 1895.

Progress in Agriculture

Historians write that agriculture began with the use of a sharp stone or stick to dig into the soil to get better yields, followed by a wooden plough and by 1000 B.C. an iron-plated plough, no longer pulled by man but by oxen and finally horses. Man only held the handles of the plough, pressing them downward so that the ploughshare would dig deeper.

In Ukraine the use of wooden farm implements lasted until the middle of the nineteenth century. Later wooden ploughs, spades and cultivators were tipped with iron for better tilling. Iron spikes were driven into wooden harrows to break the soil better. Some Ukrainians brought this equipment to Canada, but it went out of use quickly once it lost its value, being too light and weak for working the virgin soil.

The first iron plough in America was made in Illinois by the blacksmith John Deere. A double-furrow plough did not appear until 1889. At the turn of the twentieth century, steam-powered tractors came into wide use. The first two Ukrainians to operate them in Canada in 1899 were Vasyl Pillipiw and Vasyl Melnyk of Star, Alberta. Shortly thereafter, gasoline-powered tractors appeared and became popular in America. When Ukrainians celebrated their fiftieth jubilee in Canada in 1941, there were 25,000 tractors, 3,000 combines, more than 40,000 automobiles and 8,000 trucks in the Province of Alberta. Progressively, agriculture has undergone a tremendous revolution. Hard manual labour is quickly disappearing. With this should definitely disappear the pejorative term "peasant," considered to be at the bottom rung of the social scale.

The agricultural revolution of the twentieth century puts the farmer on an equal basis with other producers. A farmer today has to be educated in technical know-how because an ignoramus is incapable of operating farm machinery. The time is coming when agriculture will be considered an essential occupation for the welfare of the country and its citizens. Wherever there is a high level of culture and developed agriculture, there is prosperity and national survival is guaranteed.

~14~

A Salute to the Pioneers

Many of us are not enthusiastic about our "pioneers." We look with disdain at and smirk about our living memorials, considering them relics. An elderly grandmother in a kerchief comes along, hunched over, barely able to walk. She sits down, wiping the tears from her eyes, remembering the old days. We respond, "Ah, what do you know, old lady? That's an old story. You're old-fashioned."

The old grandmother, having wiped her tears, keeps on walking. "You children don't know how much I suffered for you," she utters. "May you never have to go through that."

Or an old man comes along, leaning on his cane, barely dragging one foot after the other. "Children, don't squander your time and money; don't waste your life daydreaming. It was not that way once. You have a house but you complain, while we lived in a shack and thanked God for even that much. You drive horses and are angry when somebody passes you in a car, while we walked a hundred miles with bread and salt on our backs to feed you, the hungry ones."

We respond, "Hey, grandpa, grandpa, that was long ago. Times have changed. Canada is a free country. We ought to get what's coming to us. We're not farm hands."

And grandpa answers, "Children, children, that's not right. We worked too hard for you and taught you too little."

Over by the road stands a small empty house behind the trees.

The white walls have turned grey and the wind has blown away the thatched roof. But I remember how, not too long ago, grandmother whitewashed the wall while grandfather fixed the hole in the roof.

Today we often scorn this vacant cottage, saying, "Why is that scarecrow standing by the road, a thorn in people's eyes? It shows that we haven't escaped our immigrant roots. It should be torn down and burned so there won't be a trace of it left."

No, sir, that is not the way. We should go to the deserted house, whitewash the walls, put on a new thatched roof and cherish it as a memorial reminding us and our children that our forefathers lived there and created good things for us from it.

There is so much of that good that a whole history could be written about it. Our fathers and grandfathers started with nothing. From their oppressed land they came empty-handed. The oppressors had given them neither education, help nor leadership. Here they started without a spoken or written knowledge of English, without a cent or any advice, only with a will as strong as steel and a complete faith in God, who heard their prayers and blessed their homes.

Let us honour that old grandmother and grandfather who provided the foundations for our work, who equipped us for life and gave us rules. Let us also salute that empty cottage—that ragged, unpainted orphan standing by the road, because that is where our ideal was born and all good things conceived.

Honour to you, dear grandpa!
Honour to you, dear grandma!
A salute to that cottage
Where you once lived,
Because from it our parents
Brought us good.
Honour to you pioneers!

Mykhailo Kozak
Ukrainskyi holos, 26 November 1941

The Fiftieth Anniversary of Ukrainian Life in Canada

When Ukrainians first came to Canada, they did not find good times. There were then no Ukrainians in Canada who could understand the English language well. For our pioneers, Canada was a strange, foreign place. There was no one to help them when they did not know the local language or customs. Those who came with families to settle on a farm had first to build a sod hut to protect themselves from the rain and wild animals. Once this was done, taking a spade brought from the Old Country, they dug up a little land for a garden where they could plant the seeds they had brought for the vegetables they would need to survive the winter.

This is what those who came in the spring did, but those who came in the fall began their life differently. Some had to cut narrow paths through impassable forests to make a way out to the nearest neighbour or railroad station. Others had to build bridges over rivers and ravines and footbridges over creeks and through swamps. And so, step by step, our pioneers progressed. Eventually they began thinking of churches, schools and community halls.

We must understand that not everything came about all at once in a single year. Far from it, all was built little by little. The pioneers suffered a lot at the beginning because they had nothing necessary for farming and had to acquire everything by hard work. Men had to go to work as labourers to earn some money to buy oxen, a cow or a horse. The women and mothers had to stay at home with the little ones, working hard clearing bush and caring for the children.

Everything has changed now, gone in a different direction. The once impassable forests have been turned into broad fields of grain, and there are no more swamps. Now we have good roads and we no longer want to drive horses or even to mention oxen. We now travel in streamlined automobiles. We have everything we need. We have educational institutions, churches, community halls and our own press. We owe it all to our pioneers, who created it through hard work and passed it on to us. My dear Ukrainian young people, since our old fathers and mothers left their native land to come to Canada to make a better life for us, let us pay our respects to our pioneers for this great service on this the fiftieth anniversary of their arrival in Canada. Let us do all we can to have festive concerts that commemorate their labour.

They spared neither effort, health nor life in their labours and so lost their youth. They have nothing left, neither their health nor their youth. Even the sweet and lovely dreams of their native land have vanished for them long ago. And long ago, they resigned themselves to the fact that this new Canadian land would become their land and a resting place for their weary bones.

Petro Lypovy
Heinsburg, Alberta
Ukrainskyi holos, 1 October 1941

On the Occasion of the Fiftieth Anniversary of Ukrainians in Canada

During the jubilee year of the fiftieth anniversary of Ukrainians in Canada, a lot was written in the Ukrainian press in Canada about the accomplishments and worth of our pioneer colonists in Western Canada. English newspapers and magazines joined in the praise. Concerts, picnics, festivals and sports competitions were held everywhere to honour the pioneers, and church services were held for those pioneers who had died.

The most elaborate celebrations commemorating Ukrainian pioneers took place in Chipman, Alberta, where Wasyl Eleniak and Mykhailo Romaniuk lived. They were two of the original pioneer "patriarchs" who began the emigration from Galicia to Canada. The former came to Canada with Ivan Pillipiw (Pylypivsky) in 1891 and the latter came in 1892. Although they first lived and worked in Gretna, Manitoba, from 1896 they lived in the Beaver Lake district of Alberta, now the town of Chipman. Both of them came from the village of Nebyliv in Kalush County, Galicia.

So that Ukrainians in Canada would celebrate the jubilee with distinction, *Ukrainskyi holos* in Winnipeg carried prior announcements. The following article appeared on 27 September 1939 under the headline "Let's Get Ready for the Fiftieth Jubilee." V. Drohaivsky suggested, among other things, that the first fifty years of Ukrainian life in Canada be documented in the form of a "history" with the following topics:

"A General Survey of Ukrainian Immigration to Canada" by the Reverend W. Kudryk of Winnipeg.

"Problems Facing Early Ukrainian Settlers in Canada," to be written by P. Svarich of Vegreville, because he knows the subject best.

"The Nature of Church and Missionary Work Among Ukrainians in Canada," about which the Basilian fathers and, in particular, Father S. Dydyk and Father N. Kryzhanovsky, both of Alberta, would be the most competent to write.

"The Russian Orthodox Mission Among Ukrainians in Canada," to be written by the Reverend P. Bozhyk of Winnipeg and the Reverend A. Chrustawka [Khrustavka] of Edmonton.

"The Protestant Movement Among Ukrainians in Canada," to be written by Mr. V. S. Plawiuk and Mr. Maksym Zalizniak, both of Edmonton.

"The Formation of Educational Associations and Other

Organizations Among Ukrainians in Canada" by T. D. Ferley of Winnipeg.

"The First Workers' Strike in Saskatchewan" by Theodore Stefanyk of Winnipeg.

"The First Ukrainian Writers in Canada" by Apolonarii Novak of Winnipeg.

"The History of the Ukrainian Press in Canada" by Myroslaw Stechishin of Winnipeg.

"Internationalism Among Ukrainian Workers in Canada" by Paul Crath and Matthew Popowich.

"The Development of Commerce Among Ukrainian Colonists in Western Canada," to be written by Ivan Semeniuk of Radway, Alberta.

"About Schools and the First Groups of Ukrainian Teachers in Canada," with J. W. Arsenych, a lawyer in Winnpeg, writing about Manitoba; Michael Stechishin, a lawyer in Yorkton, writing about Saskatchewan; and W. A. Czumer and Elias Kiriak [Iliia Kyriiak] of Edmonton writing about Alberta.

"The History of Ukrainian Boarding Schools in Canada," to be written by such former rectors as Julian Stechishin, a lawyer in Saskatoon; Peter Lazarowich [Petro Lazarovych], a lawyer in Edmonton; George Skwarok [Iurii Shkvarok], a lawyer in Mundare, Alberta, and Vasyl Teresiv, a high school teacher in Myrnam, Alberta.

"Church and Religious Struggles Among Ukrainians in Canada," to be written by Wasyl Swystun, a lawyer in Winnipeg.

"The Establishment of the Greek Orthodox Church in Canada" by the Reverend S. V. Sawchuk [Savchuk] of Winnipeg.

"Ukrainian Community Halls" by Joseph Yasenchuk [Iosef Iasenchuk] of Vancouver.

"Political Issues in Canada from the Ukrainian National Viewpoint" by Nykyta Romaniuk, a lawyer in Toronto.

"Canadian Industry and Ukrainian Immigration to Eastern Canada" by Theodore Humeniuk, a lawyer in Toronto.

"How Ukrainians Differed from Other Immigrants to Western Canada" by Dr. Datskiw [Datskiv] of Winnipeg.

"Legal Aspects of Canadian Citizenship for Ukrainians" by D. Yanda [Ianda], a lawyer in Edmonton; D. Yakimishchak [Iakymishchak], a lawyer in Winnipeg, and Dr. Ivan Yatsiw [Iatsiv], a lawyer in Windsor, Ontario.

"The Economic Achievements of Ukrainians During Their First Fifty Years in Canada," with K. Prodan, an agronomist in Winnipeg, writing about Manitoba; Savella Stechishin, a teacher of home economics in Saskatoon, writing about Saskatchewan; and William Pidruchney [Vasyl Pidruchny], an agronomist in Smoky Lake, writing about Alberta.

"The Influence of Ukrainian Professionals on the Social Life of

Ukrainians in Canada," with Dr. Ivan Verchomin [Verkhomyn] of Edmonton writing about Alberta; Dr. George Dragan [Iurii Drahan] of Saskatoon writing about Saskatchewan; and Dr. Harry [Hryhorii] Novak of Winnipeg writing about Manitoba.

"Mutual Benefit Associations and Other Ukrainian Educational Organizations," to be written by one of the older members. The same applies to "Ukrainian Women's Organizations in Canada."

The suggestion was a good one. Unfortunately, it did not stimulate any interest because not one of the above persons responded, except for the Basilian fathers, who celebrated their fortieth anniversary in Canada on 2 August 1942 in Mundare, Alberta, on which occasion they published a special memorial book about their religious work among Ukrainian Catholics in Canada.

Ukrainian Pioneers in Canada and the Change from the Julian to the Gregorian Calendar

In 1940 long articles appeared in the Ukrainian press on the topic of changing the calendar. The first person to raise the question was Mykhailo Dereniuk of Toronto. Over fifty interested contributors participated in the discussion with the majority in favour of changing from the Julian calendar (almost two weeks behind the Gregorian) used by the churches of the Greek rite to the Gregorian calendar used by the Catholic and Protestant churches.

The main argument for change was that the Julian calendar did not allow Ukrainians to celebrate important holidays with the majority of Canadian people. The leaders of the Ukrainian Orthodox church and the Russian Orthodox priests paid no attention to the voices raised in the press in favour of change. Some even accused those advocating change of treason. Without proof, they claimed that a foreign power was behind this agitation.

The priests of the Ukrainian Greek Catholic church asked their congregations to vote on it, and wherever the majority wanted a change to the Gregorian they moved their holy days to coincide with the Roman Catholic. The result can be seen in this news item on page seven of the *Kanadiiskyi farmer*, published on 23 April 1941 under the headline "Easter by the New Calendar": "In Edmonton Ukrainian Catholics celebrated this Easter by the new calendar. On the farms, half celebrated by the old calendar."

The Jubilee Year and the New Calendar

Below is a letter taken from *Ukrainski visti* [Ukrainian News], Edmonton, Alberta, 22 April 1941:

Chipman, Alberta

We have been waiting a long time for the moment when we could celebrate our holidays with the rest of the civilized world. And this moment has arrived together with the jubilee of Ukrainian immigration to Canada. This is a new step forward in this new epoch of our history here in Canada. With this new calendar we have begun a new period in our history, just as fifty years ago we began a new settlement in a new world. We are pioneering for a second time.

When we were leaving the Old Country there were those who tried to frighten us about Canada by saying that there was no future for us here. But we did not listen to them. We went and began a new life in Canada. We did not regret this and we even expect that from here we will be able to help our native land. It is the same for those who do not listen to people who frighten them with Latinization or with some wolf in the woods, and accept the new calendar for the future good of their children.

We hope that in this jubilee year all Ukrainians, regardless of their faith and organization, will accept this new calendar for the good and glory of their people.

Ukrainian Pioneers of Chipman, Alberta.

Acknowledgments

The following people encouraged the author to publish this book about Ukrainian pioneers in Canada: Nykolai Buk, formerly a teacher, then a manager of a service station at Two Hills, Alberta; Michael Ponich [Mykhailo Ponych], a lawyer at Two Hills; Nick Dowhaniuk [Nykolai Dovhaniuk], a storekeeper at Two Hills; Parania Lupul, a homeowner in Edmonton; Mykhailina Sharyk, a storekeeper in Calder, Alberta; William N. Huculak [Vasyl Hutsuliak], a native of Borivtsi, Bukovyna, and a pioneer storekeeper at Willingdon, Alberta; Harry Worobets [Hryhorii Vorobets], a pioneer farmer at Andrew, Alberta; Pavlo Harapniuk, a pioneer settler in Dalmure, Alberta; Pavlo Moroz, a section foreman in Smoky Lake, Alberta; Kost Romaniuk, a postmaster in Smoky Lake; Ivan Zelenko, a storekeeper and postmaster at Edwand, Alberta; Andrii Shewchuk [Shevchuk], a manager of a hardware store in Bellis, Alberta; Akhtemii Zavadiuk, a section foreman in Spedden, Alberta; Vasyl Andrusiak, a farmer and storekeeper at Elk Point, Alberta; Petro Mamchur, a carpenter in Elk Point; Joseph Kuziw [Iosef Kuziv], a pioneer farmer in Prumula, Alberta; Semion Evchyn, a pioneer farmer in Northern Valley, Alberta; Ivan Kobylnyk, a storekeeper in Derwent, Alberta; Steve [Stefan] Mulka, the municipal secretary in Myrnam, Alberta; Peter S. Dubetz [Petro Dubets], a storekeeper and farmer at Smoky Lake; Steve Samycia [Stefan Samytsia], a masseur at Radway, Alberta; Iliia Wakaruk [Vakaruk], a retired farmer in Wahstao, Alberta; Vasyl Saldan, a blacksmith and mechanic at Elk Point; Pavlo Buk, a truck driver in Heinsburg, Alberta; Dmytro Makowichuk [Makoviichuk], a storekeeper in Myrnam.

Postscript

In the preface, the author indicated that this is neither a work of literature nor history, but simply ordinary recollections. So if this book has spelling and grammatical errors or if the dates and events mentioned in it are inaccurate, this should not detract from the author's purpose or good will.

These recollections were collected and written down as accurately as was possible from the author's personal acquaintance with the events or experiences and the reliability of the information he received from other people. They were written impartially and without the least prejudice.

These recollections were written in memory of all those Ukrainian settlers who lived through the earliest pioneer period and contributed in whatever way to the development of our future in this new country. Whether in the economic, educational, cultural, social, religious or commercial fields, all are valuable memories for us and, I believe, worth remembering forever.

A lot of space was taken up in this book by matters of a social nature—church, school, organization and politics. In fact, these matters belong to history and someday someone will write about them better and in more detail. These recollections are only an outline, but our pioneer settlers met the same situation in every part of Western Canada and everywhere they began a new life in a new environment by doing the best they could, and so these recollections come to resemble a history.

The author calls this book "recollections" because they remind us of those distant, pioneer times experienced by every Ukrainian pioneer in Canada. They focus mainly on the first twenty-five years of Ukrainian life in Canada—on the immigration that took place before the war in Europe. They were also written to leave something for our descendants, so that in their leisure moments they might think about their forefathers.

Efforts were made to acquire photographs of those first Ukrainian settlers of the three Prairie provinces, but they did not succeed because at that time our people did not take photographs or think about memoirs.

An Outline of Historical and Ordinary Occurrences from 1492 to 1942

1492   The discovery of America by Christopher Columbus and the beginning of communication across the Atlantic Ocean.

1497   John Cabot discovers Newfoundland and the shores of Nova Scotia.

1534   Jacques Cartier discovers the Gulf of St. Lawrence in Canada.

1605   Samuel de Champlain discovers the Indian settlements of Stadacona and Hochelaga on the banks of the St. Lawrence River in Canada.

1606   The arrival of the first French settlers in Nova Scotia.

1607   The first group of English colonists known as the Puritans arrive in Virginia.

1608   Samuel de Champlain founds Quebec, the first town in Canada.

1627   Cardinal Richelieu organizes the "Hundred Associates," a commercial group of Europeans operating in Canada.

1663   Eastern Canada comes under the formal rule of France.

1667   The Hudson's Bay Company receives a charter from the king of England to trade with the Indians in northern Canada.

1713   The Seven Years' War between France and England ends with the Treaty of Utrecht by which Nova Scotia comes under English control.

1751   The first white man, M. de Niverville, a Frenchman, visits the Canadian West.

1754   Anthony Henday, an Englishman, is the first to trade with the Indians in Alberta.

1759   The English-French battle near Quebec for American possessions.

1763   The Treaty of Paris by which France surrenders Canada to England.

1774   The beginning of the rebellion of the American colonists against England.

1776   On 4 July the United States of America declares its independence from England and George Washington becomes the first president.

1780   The beginning of accelerated colonization of Canada by the British.

1791   The division of Canada into Upper and Lower Canada.

1793   Alexander Mackenzie becomes the first to discover the far western territories of northern Canada.

1794   The discovery of Vancouver Island by the English captain, Vancouver.

1806   The French woman, Marie-Anne Gaboury, is the first white woman in Western Canada. In 1807 she married B. Lagemodière and had a daughter who was the mother of the Indian leader, Louis Riel, who led an Indian rebellion in Western Canada against the Canadian government in 1869 and 1885.

1812-14   A war between the United States of America and the British army in the eastern colonies of Canada.

1813   Lord Selkirk attempts the first colonization of the Province of Manitoba with Scots.

1822   The French missionary, Father Provencher, founds the Roman Catholic mission in Manitoba.

1825   A. West founds the first Anglican mission in Manitoba in the St. John district of Winnipeg.

1834   The building of the first railroad in the United States.

1837   The first railroad in Eastern Canada.

1838   A great uprising in Quebec between the French and English peoples; that is, between Lower and Upper Canada.

1842   The appearance of the first Roman Catholic missionaries among the Indians of Alberta.

1845   Fort Edmonton and district has a population of 130 white settlers and half-breeds.

1848   The first vegetable garden in British Columbia is planted in the Vancouver area.

1852   John Black founds the first Presbyterian church in Winnipeg.

1862   The first colonists in Kamloops, B.C., were the Schuberts, who set out from Winnipeg in ox-drawn wagons for the long journey across the plains and mountains in search of gold. Among them was the mother of the three Schubert boys.

1865   Ahapii Honcharenko, who lived near San Francisco, is the first Ukrainian in America.

1867   The British North America Act unites the Canadian provinces into a federation. John A. Macdonald becomes the first prime minister.

1867   The coronation of Queen Victoria.

1869   The first Indian uprising breaks out in the Red River valley in Manitoba.

1870   Manitoba joins the Dominion of Canada.

1872   MacDougall, the first Methodist missionary in Alberta, perishes in a snowstorm while returning to Edmonton from the mission in Calgary.

1873   Construction begins on the Canadian Pacific Railway.

1874   German Mennonites from Russia become the first colonists in southern Manitoba.

1877   The first ranchers known as cowboys appear in Western Canada.

1878   The first French farm settlement in Alberta is founded at St. Albert, ten miles north of Edmonton.

1878   The first Icelanders settle in Dufferin and Gimli, Manitoba.

1880   Winnipeg is connected by rail to the east and south.

1881   The discovery of the first coal mine in Western Canada on the banks of the Belly River near Lethbridge, Alberta.

1882   Western Canada is divided into four districts: Assiniboia, Alberta, Athabasca and Saskatchewan, with Regina as the administrative capital.

1883   The Farmers' Union, the first farmers' organization in Western Canada, is formed in Brandon, Manitoba.

1885   Drought strikes the West and the Indians rebel in Saskatchewan.

1886   On 28 June the first passenger train leaves Halifax for Vancouver.

1886   Germans from Hungary become the first colonists to farm in Saskatchewan, settling in the Langenburg and Hohenhoe districts.

1887   The first English colonists in Alberta settle in the Sturgeon River district.

1889   The first German colonists in Alberta settle at Gleichen.

1891   The first Ukrainians come to Canada: Ivan Pillipiw "Pylypivsky" and Wasyl Eleniak from Halychyna and Nykola Koroliuk from Bessarabia.

1892   The first Ukrainians to settle with their families in Canada are Vasyl Iatsiv, Mykhailo Romaniuk, Iosef Paish, A. Paish, Nykola Tychkovsky and M. Eleniak.

1893   Franko Iatsiv, the son of Vasyl and Mariia Iatsiv, is the first Ukrainian boy born in Canada on 14 February 1893 in Winnipeg.

1894   The founding of the Ukrainian colony at Beaver Creek, Alberta.

1895   Dr. Joseph Oleskiw of Lviv in Galicia visits Ukrainians in America and Canada.

1896   The first Ukrainian colonies in Manitoba are founded at Brokenhead, Gonor, Stuartburn and Dauphin, and in Saskatchewan at Grenfell.

1897   Larger colonies of Ukrainians founded at Fish Creek and Crooked Lake, now Wakaw, Saskatchewan.

1897   School District 412 at Limestone Lake, Alberta, becomes the first school district among Ukrainians in Western Canada.

1897   The Reverend D. Romanov and Deacon V. Alexandrov are the first Russian missionaries among Ukrainians in Canada.

1897   The first Ukrainian Greek Catholic Divine Liturgy in Canada is celebrated by the Reverend Nestor Dmytriw in Stuartburn, Manitoba, and later at Limestone Lake School in Alberta.

1897   The beginning of mass emigration of Ukrainians from Europe to Canada.

1898   Over two hundred Ukrainian families arrive in the Hawaiian Islands.

1898   Building commences on the first Ukrainian Greek Catholic church in Canada at Star, Alberta.

1899   Theodore Nemirsky becomes the first Ukrainian postmaster in Canada at Wostok, Alberta.

1899   Vasyl Pillipiw and Vasyl Melnyk are the first Ukrainians to learn to operate steam tractors.

1901   The beginning of church conflict among the Ukrainian colonists in Western Canada.

1901   Fourth census in Canada lists Ukrainians as "Galician," "Russian," "Bukovinian," "Austrian," "Ruthenian" and "Polish."

1902   The Basilian fathers, the first Ukrainian Greek Catholic missionaries, arrive in Alberta.

1902   The first Ukrainian newspaper, *Kanadiiskyi farmer*, edited by Ivan Negrich, appears in Winnipeg.

1903   "Bishop" Seraphim and the beginning of Protestantism among Ukrainian colonists in Canada.

1905   "Zerebko [Zherebko] and Turcheniuk" of Sifton, Manitoba, is the first company founded by Ukrainians.

1905   The first Ukrainian bookstore "Doiachek" opens on Selkirk Avenue in Winnipeg.

1905   V. Karpets and N. Hladky organize the Brotherhood of St. Nicholas at the Basilian church in Winnipeg.

1906   The first concert in honour of Taras Shevchenko is held by the students of the Ruthenian Training School in the Manitoba Hall on Logan Avenue in Winnipeg.

1906   The Canadian National Railway reaches Edmonton and the University of Alberta is opened.

1907   The first Ukrainian-English teachers' convention is held in the Labour Hall at Manitoba and Power Streets in Winnipeg.

1908   The congregation of the Ukrainian Greek Catholic Church of Saints Vladimir and Olha begin construction of the first Ukrainian school at Stella and MacGregor in Winnipeg.

1908   The 300th anniversary of the founding of Quebec and the visit of the Prince of Wales to Canada.

1908   The brothers, Koziar and V. Khraplyvy, organize the first Ukrainian reading club in Ladywood, Manitoba.

1909   Father Sozon Dydyk, a Ukrainian Greek Catholic priest, attends a Roman Catholic congress in Quebec City.

1909   The third convention of the Ukrainian-English teachers of Manitoba and Saskatchewan is held at the Tomko Yastremsky [Iastremsky] Hall on Stella Avenue in Winnipeg and the establishment of the Ukrainian

Publishing Company.

1909   The French priest, Father Sabourin, inaugurates the first boarding house for Ukrainian boys in Sifton, Manitoba.

1909   Pavlo Melnyk and V. Romaniuk organize the first reading club among the Ukrainian colonists of Myrnam, Alberta.

1910   W. A. Czumer and T. D. Ferley buy a printing press for the Ukrainian Publishing Company in Winnipeg and begin publishing the *Ukrainskyi holos* newspaper with T. D. Ferley as its first editor.

1910   Theodore Stefanyk is appointed school organizer among Ukrainians in Manitoba.

1910   Paul Rudyk and Peter Svarich organize the Ukrainian National Co-operative in Vegreville, Alberta.

1910   Andrii Sheptytsky, metropolitan of the Ukrainian Greek Catholic church in Galicia, visits Canada for the first time.

1910   The Edmonton branch of the Ukrainian socialists establishes the *Nova hromada* [New Community] newspaper, which appears weekly for three years.

1911   Sir Wilfrid Laurier's Liberal government is defeated over reciprocity.

1911   The socialist Vasyl Holovatsky, who is the first Ukrainian to run for Parliament, receives 146 votes in the Selkirk riding of Manitoba.

1911   Under pressure from Ukrainian politicians, the governments of Saskatchewan and Alberta open "Schools for Foreigners" in Regina and Vegreville, modelled after the Ruthenian Training School of Manitoba.

1912   Joseph Megas and Petro Shvydky found the short-lived newspaper, *Novyi krai* [New Country], in Rosthern, Saskatchewan.

1912   Bishop Nykyta Budka of Galicia is appointed bishop for Ukrainian Catholics in Canada.

1913   Roman Kremar publishes the newspaper *Novyny* [The News] in Edmonton.

1913   The first mass rally of Ukrainians is held in Chipman [Vegreville], Alberta.

1913   Andrew Shandro of Whitford, Alberta, becomes the first Ukrainian MLA.

1913   John R. Boyle, Minister of Education for Alberta, persecutes Ukrainian teachers who participated in the election campaign.

1913   The taxpayers of Bukowina School District build a private school in defiance of Mr. Boyle's orders.

1913   Harry Michalyshyn and Nykolai Andriiv reorganize the Markiian Shashkevych reading club in Edmonton to increase its activities and build a community hall in Edmonton.

1914   The outbreak of the First World War.

1914   Theodore Stefanyk becomes the first Ukrainian city councillor in Winnipeg.

1914   The editors of *Novyny* carry on a polemic with J. R. Boyle over the bilingual school system among Ukrainians in Alberta.

1914   M. Belegay and W. A. Czumer organize "The Ukrainian Beneficial Association" in Alberta, which lasts until 1922, when it is disbanded and the money returned to the members.

1915   Dmytro Ferbey purchases the Ukrainian Book Store from *Novyny*, which he has managed successfully to this day.

1915   The first Ukrainian workingman's self-education society is organized in Edmonton. Its members later become Bolsheviks.

1915   Paul Crath, a prominent socialist and internationalist organizer of the Ukrainian workers in Canada, is ordained a Presbyterian minister in Toronto.

1915   The first Ukrainian teachers' convention is held in Edmonton.

1915   M. Dorosh organizes the Ukrainian travelling theatre in Western Canada with N. Babii and Emiliia Chychka of Edmonton in the lead roles.

1916   T. D. Ferley is the first Ukrainian MLA elected in Manitoba.

1916   The Petro Mohyla Ukrainian Institute opens in Saskatchewan with Wasyl Swystun as its first rector and Joseph Megas chairman of the board.

1916   The Liberal party comes to power in all three Prairie provinces and the bilingual public school system comes to an end in Western Canada.

1917   Toma Tomashevsky, publisher of the Ukrainian newspaper *Postup* [Progress] in Mundare, Alberta, encourages Ukrainians to join the United Farmers of Alberta.

1917   Ukrainians in Vegreville organize the Taras Shevchenko boarding school.

1917   The Ukrainian Greek Catholic community hall opens in Edmonton.

1918   Wasyl Swystun and the Reverend Dr. I. German organize the Ukrainian Orthodox Brotherhood Association in Canada. The first congregations are formed at Sitch, Kolomea, Suchava and Shepyntsi, Alberta.

1918   The opening of the Mykhailo Hrushevsky Ukrainian Institute in the Caledonia Hotel on 98th Street in Edmonton with A. T. Kibzey as its first rector.

1918   The First World War ends on 11 November.

1919   Sir Wilfrid Laurier, a long-time prime minister of Canada, dies on 7 February.

1919   The first labour strike in Winnipeg.

1920   The first session of the League of Nations is held in Geneva.

1921   Ukrainians in Canada send Joseph Megas and I. Petrushevich [Petrushevych] to Europe to lobby the British to support the creation of a Ukrainian state in Europe.

1921   The United Farmers of Alberta come to power. Vasyl Fedun and M. Chornohuz are two Ukrainians elected as MLAs.

1922   The first group of "Ukrainian" communists leaves Winnipeg for Russia.

1923   Smoky Lake, Alberta, is the only town in Canada whose entire council is composed of members of Ukrainian extraction.

1923   Dr. John [Ivan] Orobko of Edmonton is the first Ukrainian doctor.

1925   The union of the English Protestant churches into the United Church of Canada.

1926   Michael Luchkovich becomes the first Ukrainian MP in Canada, elected to represent Vegreville.

1927   A bumper crop in Western Canada and good prices.

1928   Vasyl Avramenko propagates Ukrainian folk dancing in Canada.

1929   Beginning of the financial crisis in Canada that lasts ten years.

1930-1   Money is scarce among Canadian farmers with wheat selling for twelve to eighteen cents per bushel.

1932-3   Bankruptcy hits farmers and small businessmen in Canada.

1932-3   Bolsheviks organize a "Hunger March" in Alberta with people walking from the rural settlements to Edmonton, where they are dispersed by club-wielding police.

1934   Farm produce becomes worthless with a dozen eggs selling for four cents, a pig for two to four cents a pound and cattle for a penny a pound, etc.

1935   Social Credit comes to power in Alberta.

1936   Cities in Western Canada become deserted as workers abandon the homes on which they can no longer afford to pay taxes and scatter to the farms. Those who stay are kept on relief.

1937   Japan attacks China without declaring war and Europe prepares feverishly for the Second World War.

1938   The Ukrainian Orthodox church consistory and the "Sobor" church congregation of Winnpeg are locked in a court battle.

1940   All of Ukraine with the exception of the Trans-Carpathian region comes under Russian occupation.

1941   Ukrainians of Canada celebrate the jubilee of their fiftieth anniversary in Canada.

1942   The German army overruns Ukraine, reaching the Caucasus Mountains and the Volga River, where the great battle of Stalingrad is fought.

1942   At the end of the year, these recollections were being prepared for publication.

Index